SELF-LEARNING MANAGEMENT SERIES

PUBLISI...

BRAND MANAGEMENT ESSENTIALS

YOU ALWAYS WANTED TO KNOW

A practical guide to building, positioning, and managing a brand that drives measurable business results.

SONIA SCROCCHI

BRAND MANAGEMENT ESSENTIALS YOU ALWAYS WANTED TO KNOW

First Edition

Published by Vibrant Publishers LLC, USA, www.vibrantpublishers.com

Paperback ISBN 13: 978-1-63651-559-5
Ebook ISBN 13: 978-1-63651-560-1
Hardback ISBN 13: 978-1-63651-561-8

Library of Congress Control Number: 2025940604

This publication is designed to provide accurate and authoritative information regarding the subject matter covered. The Author have made every effort in the preparation of this book to ensure the accuracy of the information. However, information in this book is sold without warranty, either expressed or implied. The Authors or the Publisher will not be liable for any damages caused or alleged to be caused either directly or indirectly by this book.

All trademarks and registered trademarks mentioned in this publication are the property of their respective owners. These trademarks are used for editorial and educational purposes only, without intent to infringe upon any trademark rights. This publication is independent and has not been authorized, endorsed, or approved by any trademark owner.

Vibrant Publishers' books are available at special quantity discounts for sales promotions, or for use in corporate training programs. For more information, please write to bulkorders@vibrantpublishers.com

Please email feedback/corrections (technical, grammatical, or spelling) to spellerrors@vibrantpublishers.com

Vibrant publishes in a variety of print and electronic formats and by print-on-demand. Some material included with standard print versions of this book may not be included in e-books or in print-on-demand. To access the complete catalog of Vibrant Publishers, visit www.vibrantpublishers.com

Exclusive Online Resources for You

As our valued reader, your purchase of this book includes access to exclusive online resources designed to enhance your learning experience. These resources can be downloaded from our website, www.vibrantpublishers.com, and are created to help you apply Brand Management concepts effectively.

Online resources for this book include the following:

1. Brand Identity Prism Worksheet
2. Brand Positioning Statement Builder
3. SWOT Analysis Template
4. Customer Persona Builder
5. Brand Charter Worksheet
6. SMART Goal Planner for Brand Managers

Why these online resources are valuable:

- **Hands-on learning:** Complex branding concepts become clearer when applied directly. These tools turn theory into actionable strategy.

- **Practical, step-by-step templates:** Each resource guides you through key brand-building processes, whether you're running a solo project or leading a cross-functional team.

- **Real-world application:** These tools reflect the workflows and templates used by professionals in agencies, startups, and enterprise teams.

- **Professional edge:** Build a portfolio of completed templates to showcase your skills—or use them directly in your next brand campaign or internal workshop.

How to access your online resources:

1. **Visit the website:** Go to www.vibrantpublishers.com
2. **Find your book:** Navigate to the book's product page via the "Shop" menu or by searching for the book title in the search bar.
3. **Request the resources:** Scroll down to the "Request Sample Book/Online Resource" section.
4. **Enter your details:** Enter your preferred email ID and select "Online Resource" as the resource type. Lastly, select "user type" and submit the request.
5. **Check your inbox:** The resources will be delivered directly to your email.

Alternatively, for quick access: simply scan the QR code below to go directly to the product page and request the online resources by filling in the required details.

https://bit.ly/bm-slm

Happy learning!

SELF-LEARNING MANAGEMENT SERIES

TITLE	PAPERBACK* ISBN

BUSINESS AND ENTREPRENEURSHIP

TITLE	PAPERBACK* ISBN
BUSINESS COMMUNICATION ESSENTIALS	9781636511634
BUSINESS ETHICS ESSENTIALS	9781636513324
BUSINESS LAW ESSENTIALS	9781636511702
BUSINESS PLAN ESSENTIALS	9781636511214
BUSINESS STRATEGY ESSENTIALS	9781949395778
ENTREPRENEURSHIP ESSENTIALS	9781636511603
INTERNATIONAL BUSINESS ESSENTIALS	9781636513294
PRINCIPLES OF MANAGEMENT ESSENTIALS	9781636511542

COMPUTER SCIENCE AND TECHNOLOGY

TITLE	PAPERBACK* ISBN
BLOCKCHAIN ESSENTIALS	9781636513003
CYBERSECURITY ESSENTIALS	9781636514888
MACHINE LEARNING ESSENTIALS	9781636513775
PYTHON ESSENTIALS	9781636512938

DATA SCIENCE FOR BUSINESS

TITLE	PAPERBACK* ISBN
BUSINESS ANALYTICS ESSENTIALS	9781636514154
BUSINESS INTELLIGENCE ESSENTIALS	9781636513362
DATA ANALYTICS ESSENTIALS	9781636511184

FINANCIAL LITERACY AND ECONOMICS

TITLE	PAPERBACK* ISBN
COST ACCOUNTING & MANAGEMENT ESSENTIALS	9781636511030
FINANCIAL ACCOUNTING ESSENTIALS	9781636510972
FINANCIAL MANAGEMENT ESSENTIALS	9781636511009
MACROECONOMICS ESSENTIALS	9781636511818
MICROECONOMICS ESSENTIALS	9781636511153
PERSONAL FINANCE ESSENTIALS	9781636511849
PRINCIPLES OF ECONOMICS ESSENTIALS	9781636512334

*Also available in Hardback & Ebook formats

SELF-LEARNING MANAGEMENT SERIES

TITLE	PAPERBACK* ISBN

HR, DIVERSITY, AND ORGANIZATIONAL SUCCESS

DIVERSITY, EQUITY, AND INCLUSION ESSENTIALS	9781636512976
DIVERSITY IN THE WORKPLACE ESSENTIALS	9781636511122
HR ANALYTICS ESSENTIALS	9781636510347
HUMAN RESOURCE MANAGEMENT ESSENTIALS	9781949395839
ORGANIZATIONAL BEHAVIOR ESSENTIALS	9781636512303
ORGANIZATIONAL DEVELOPMENT ESSENTIALS	9781636511481

LEADERSHIP AND PERSONAL DEVELOPMENT

DECISION MAKING ESSENTIALS	9781636510026
INCLUSIVE LEADERSHIP ESSENTIALS	9781636514765
INDIA'S ROAD TO TRANSFORMATION: WHY LEADERSHIP MATTERS	9781636512273
LEADERSHIP ESSENTIALS	9781636510316
TIME MANAGEMENT ESSENTIALS	9781636511665

MODERN MARKETING AND SALES

CONSUMER BEHAVIOR ESSENTIALS	9781636513263
DIGITAL MARKETING ESSENTIALS	9781949395747
MARKETING MANAGEMENT ESSENTIALS	9781636511788
MARKET RESEARCH ESSENTIALS	9781636513744
MODERN ADVERTISING ESSENTIALS	9781636514857
SALES MANAGEMENT ESSENTIALS	9781636510743
SERVICES MARKETING ESSENTIALS	9781636511733
SOCIAL MEDIA MARKETING ESSENTIALS	9781636512181

*Also available in Hardback & Ebook formats

SELF-LEARNING MANAGEMENT SERIES

TITLE	PAPERBACK* ISBN
OPERATIONS MANAGEMENT	
AGILE ESSENTIALS	9781636510057
OPERATIONS & SUPPLY CHAIN MANAGEMENT ESSENTIALS	9781949395242
PRODUCT MANAGEMENT ESSENTIALS	9781636514796
PROJECT MANAGEMENT ESSENTIALS	9781636510712
STAKEHOLDER ENGAGEMENT ESSENTIALS	9781636511511

CURRENT AFFAIRS

DIGITAL SHOCK	9781636513805

*Also available in Hardback & Ebook formats

About the Author

Sonia Scrocchi is a Canadian brand strategy consultant whose career is defined by one consistent aim: to turn thoughtful strategy into measurable marketplace advantage. Armed with a Master of Arts Degree in Luxury Brand Management from Regent's University London and a Master of Business Administration specializing in Business Analytics from Hult International Business School, she approaches every brief with equal parts quantitative discipline and a deep appreciation for the power of storytelling to move people. Her earlier academic endeavors, including a Bachelor of Commerce and a Postgraduate Diploma both in Marketing Management, laid the foundation she still relies on today.

For more than a decade, Sonia has worked directly with founders, in-house teams, and C-suite leaders across various industries, including luxury fashion, real estate, publishing, software, energy, retail, and transportation. Her projects routinely span multiple continents and time zones, demanding cultural sensitivity as well as analytical rigor. That global perspective has taught her to decode subtle shifts in consumer belief systems and to adapt a single brand promise into languages, images, and experiences that resonate from market to market.

An analytical mindset is the backbone of her practice. Clear hypotheses, disciplined measurement, and straightforward conclusions ensure that insight, rather than intuition, steers every creative choice. By weaving classic luxury principles such as craftsmanship, scarcity, and elevation into evidence-based strategy, she delivers programs that are both distinctive and defensible, giving clients confidence that bold ideas can still withstand close scrutiny.

Results remain paramount. Sonia has led initiatives that delivered double-digit increases in brand awareness, improved marketing ROI through data-driven budget allocation, and supported successful acquisition exits by strengthening product narratives. Her strategic contributions have been recognized with industry awards for excellence, yet she measures success primarily by the clarity and longevity of the brands that emerge from her work.

Writing this guide was the next logical step: a chance to distill her unique experience and approach into a practical framework that future brand builders and business achievers can apply from day one.

What Experts Say About This Book!

With emerging brands from China, India, and beyond reshaping global markets, like BYD, On Shoes, Tata, and even bold moves from legacy players like Jaguar, understanding brand strategy has never been more critical. *Brand Management Essentials* offers a timely and practical guide to building, positioning, and growing brands in this competitive world. After all, creating a brand is paramount to all successful businesses!

– Pablo Ibarreche Luquin,
Business Consultant

Is everybody in the world as mystified by the idea of brands and branding as I am? If so, *Brand Management Essentials* will get you started on a whole new way of looking at not only branding but also your use of it to increase your business.

– Mike Michelsen,
Writer & Journalist

Brand Management Essentials provides readers a top-to-bottom framework that shows why your brand is your most valuable asset. If you're looking for an in-depth exploration of key branding concepts in an approachable, easy-to-read style, this book is for you.

– Jamie Turner,
Author, Professor, and CNN Contributor

Brand Management Essentials is a clear and practical roadmap that shows how strong brand thinking can guide identity, equity, and strategy at every stage of business growth.

– Prof. Filippo Marchesani,
Professor of "Management of Innovation" and "Digital Consumer Behavior", University "G. d'Annunzio" Chieti-Pescara.

What Experts Say About This Book!

Brand Management Essentials delivers a practical roadmap for turning brand strategy into measurable business impact by blending foundational principles with actionable tools for identity, segmentation, and market adaptability. The chapters are refreshing, and the inclusion of neuromarketing and the science behind branding sets this book apart from your typical branding books.

– Michelle Bartonico,
Senior Strategist, Trinity University

Brand Management Essentials is a no-nonsense guide for anyone building a purposeful brand in today's dynamic, real-world markets. It reads like wisdom from a seasoned brand builder who provides clear, practical and immediately applicable frameworks for navigating the messy reality of growing brands where it matters most.

– Maria Isa,
Founder, AfriMaisha Marketing

Table of Contents

Preface

Brand conversations once belonged almost solely to the marketing department. Now they influence businesses in multiple facets, from hiring pitches, investor decks, and even product roadmaps. I wrote this book to give students and professionals a concise, practical map of that expanded territory and to demonstrate that a solid grounding in brand management benefits anyone – entrepreneur or employee, in any industry.

The chapters trace the life cycle of a living brand: defining identity, choosing audiences, building equity, measuring performance, and adjusting course as culture or technology shifts. Each section couples a clear framework with ready-to-use worksheets and diagnostics, tools you can drop straight into a weekly planning session.

Three convictions guide the material:

1. **Essential knowledge, universal gain:** A working grasp of awareness, loyalty, and equity sharpens everyday decisions for founders, product managers, analysts, and designers alike.

2. **Shared language multiplies impact:** When everyone on a team understands the same core concepts, briefings run faster, goals align, and creative ideas survive the journey, from whiteboard to market.

3. **Adaptability is a core skill:** Markets move at the speed of a scroll. The Brand Agility Loop shows how disciplined iteration keeps you relevant without sacrificing strategic focus.

Read the book cover-to-cover or jump straight to the chapter that matches today's challenge. If these pages help you craft a sharper value proposition, defend a budget with confidence, or catch an early warning sign before competitors do, they have done their job.

Brand management essentials are career essentials. Master them, and you will add value in any organization, now and throughout your professional life.

Introduction to the Book

Brands compete for attention in every marketplace, yet most managers still treat "brand" as a slogan or a splash of color rather than the operating system of the business. This book makes a different claim: brand thinking belongs at the center of every strategic conversation. Whether you are launching a side-hustle, steering a mature enterprise, or advising clients, the concepts that follow will help you create value that survives price wars, copy-cats, and shifting consumer moods.

The chapters mirror a brand's natural life cycle. We begin with foundations: clarifying identity, awareness, and reputation, then move to customer insight and segmentation, where you will learn to turn data into empathy. From there, you will build a sustainable identity, craft positioning, and explore the neuroscience that links emotion to choice. Later chapters show how experience design and cross-channel communication convert strategy into reality, before the final section connects performance metrics to day-to-day decisions. Each step equips readers with practical tools that they can apply hands-on to their unique business scenarios.

A solid grasp of brand management does more than polish a logo. It anchors product development, guides hiring, aligns budgets, and acts as a compass when markets tilt. Teams that share a common vocabulary, equity, loyalty, and purpose move faster because debates focus on evidence, not opinion. Leaders who understand brand signals can read early warnings in social chatter long before they surface in quarterly numbers. In short, mastering the essentials strengthens every link between vision and profit. By the final chapter, you will be able to:

- Design a brand identity that resonates across cultures and channels.
- Segment audiences with precision and craft value propositions that speak to real pain points.
- Build experiences that move customers from first glance to lasting advocacy.
- Diagnose brand health using metrics that executives respect and investors trust.
- Respond to market shifts with confidence, knowing which assets to defend and which to reinvent.

Entrepreneurs who need to stretch every dollar, product owners chasing product-market fit, analysts translating dashboards into direction, creatives selling bold ideas to cautious stakeholders, any professional who touches the customer experience will find tools here to raise the quality of their contribution and the clarity of team dialogue.

These pages will not bury you in jargon or abstract theory. Instead, they aim to bridge the gap between classroom models and the messy realities of budget constraints, cross-functional politics, and relentless competition. Put the frameworks to work, adapt them to your context, and you will forge brands that outlast trends and earn a place in people's lives.

Who Can Benefit From This Book?

1. Entrepreneurs and founders who need a fast, practical way to shape a distinctive market position and make every marketing dollar count.

2. Mid-level executives and team leads, responsible for translating brand strategy into day-to-day decisions across product, sales, or customer experience.

3. Marketing-adjacent professionals, from designers to analysts, seeking a shared vocabulary that links their work to awareness, loyalty, and long-term equity.

4. Learners and career switchers in higher education, executive education, or upskilling programs who want a concise, field-tested primer on brand management essentials.

How to Use This Book?

This book is organized so you can either work through it methodically or dip into the parts most relevant to you right now.

If it's your first time exploring brand management:

Start at Chapter 1 and move straight through. Each chapter layers fundamentals: identity, segmentation, positioning, and measurement, so you finish with a complete framework.

If you're a curious learner, an ambitious professional, or an entrepreneur:

Use the book as a reference guide. Keep the following shortcuts in mind as you apply the material:

- Need sharper positioning? Turn to Chapters 3-4
- Planning customer touchpoints? See Chapter 6 on experience design.
- Investigating flagging loyalty or unclear ROI? Consult Chapters 7-8 for metrics and the Brand Agility Loop.

To turn the material into action, follow these practical steps:

1. **Apply concepts to a live brand as you read:**
   Keep your own venture, employer, or a favorite label in mind. Drop each model onto that example to see immediately where gaps or opportunities emerge.

2. **Use the end-of-chapter key points for quick refreshers:**
   Before a meeting or presentation, flip to the summary box at the chapter's close for a fast reminder of core terms and recommended actions.

3. **Revisit sections as markets shift:**
   Brand strategy is iterative. When new competitors
   appear or customer needs change, return to the identity
   and measurement chapters to recalibrate.

Read cover-to-cover or consult it on demand. The material is
designed to turn essential brand theory into clear, confident
decisions that advance ventures, teams, and careers.

CHAPTER **1**

Introduction to Brand Management

Key Learning Objectives

- Define a brand and identify its core components.
- Outline the primary responsibilities of a brand manager.
- Describe the brand journey from awareness to customer loyalty.
- Distinguish the difference between brand awareness, identity, and reputation.
- Understand the importance of purpose-driven branding in today's markets.

Brand management has an incredible impact on a company's success, more so than you may realize. A brand has the potential to be a company's greatest asset when executed effectively or its biggest weakness if neglected. Before understanding why brand management matters, you must understand what a brand is.

Essentially, a brand is the sum of every interaction and story tied to an entity. It can be connected to the feeling and perception that lingers in a customer's mind long after a product has been used or a service has been delivered.

For example, think of popular brands with strong brand management strategies like Apple (technology company) or Coca-Cola (beverage company), and ask yourself what comes to mind. Maybe you think "sleek and high-tech" when thinking of Apple or "crisp and refreshing" when you think of Coca-Cola. And maybe you're even thinking these things without owning any Apple products or consuming any Coca-Cola. These examples show how a strong brand combines history, quality, and imagery to leave you with a lasting impression.

FUN FACT Coca-Cola was originally marketed as a medicinal tonic in the late 1800s, and over time, due to its popularity, the brand transformed into a globally recognized household favorite. Consistent brand choices, such as the iconic glass Coca-Cola bottle and the signature red-and-white logo, helped it become one of the world's most recognizable soft drink brands.

Big names in advertising have long tried to capture the meaning of a brand. David Ogilvy, often called the "father of advertising" (Tikkanen, n.d.), famously defined a brand as "the intangible sum of a product's attributes" (Ogilvy, 1983). Some view a brand as everything, from the product itself to how it's marketed in the long term. Others emphasize the symbols and messaging that make a brand unique.

Regardless of perspective, there is no doubt that strong brands help businesses stand out. They build loyalty and can ultimately make or break a company's success.

Brand management is about creating and keeping a good image for a brand. This is achieved by using different ways to make a brand more valuable and easily recognizable over time. It is the process of building and maintaining the belief and perception of a product, service, or company in the eyes of customers and key stakeholders over time.

Building a strong brand takes careful planning. It's about ensuring that everything a company does aligns with its big-picture goals. This helps create a clear, trustworthy image for customers. To get started, businesses must be aware of all the components that make up their brand. This is crucial for establishing a strong brand identity. It's like figuring out the key ingredients in a recipe.

In this chapter, you will learn about these essential components of a successful brand. These include identity, awareness, reputation, and how they work together to build a distinctive brand. Understanding these components will help you see how a brand develops and evolves from initial recognition to customer loyalty.

We will also explore how strategic brand management builds emotional connections and provides value to consumers, ultimately distinguishing a brand from the competition. Additionally, we will discover the importance of purpose-driven branding in today's dynamic marketplace and understand how a strong brand can influence purchase decisions beyond the product itself.

You will also learn about the essential tasks and responsibilities of a brand manager, as well as gain insights into how they use strategy to build and improve a brand's image and reputation. A brand manager must understand what their customers desire and position what they offer in alignment. To effectively manage a brand, it is critical to understand the various factors that contribute to a brand's foundation. Brand managers must have a strong working knowledge of the inner workings of a brand.

Businesses spend significant time and resources building and maintaining their brands. Strong brand management drives sales and long-term growth by fostering loyalty and encouraging repeat business. Let's begin the journey of mastering brand management by diving into the essential elements that form the foundation of a strong brand.

1.1 The Foundation of a Brand

The foundation of a brand is made up of many parts. These parts work together to strengthen the brand. The brand name is one part, while the logo is another. Colors and designs are also important as they help people to recognize the brand. However, more importantly, a brand also has a personality, which refers to how it makes people feel.

The brand makes a promise to customers, which tells them what they can expect. It also comes with values that demonstrate to customers what the company believes in and stands for. These promises and values may be blatantly expressed by a company, or they may include "not-so-obvious" signals that impact customers' perceptions of the company subliminally. Regardless, it's important to remember that a critical factor that forms the foundation of a brand is how that brand resonates in a customer's mind to build emotional recall.

When similar products or services compete for attention, the brand name or logo could be what encourages a customer to choose one product over another. However, it's important to consider what it is about that brand name or logo that influenced the customer's decision. The customer likely had a preconceived impression or belief about that brand that led them to choose it. For example, consider two popular brands of dish soap: Dawn and Palmolive. Dawn is known for its emotional commercials about saving wildlife. On the other hand, Palmolive's message indicates that it will soften your hands while you do the dishes.

Now, think about the last time you shopped for dish soap. Can you remember what made you choose one brand over another? Did you walk down the household cleaning aisle and grab the same brand as always without much consideration? If so, perhaps you're more loyal to that brand than you realize, relying on the familiar choice without questioning it. Or maybe you paused to evaluate your options. If so, what influenced your decision? Was it a bold claim on the label, a promise of better results, or something more subtle? Did one brand present itself as environmentally friendly, like Dawn, aligning with your sustainability and animal care values? Or did another brand seem like the option you deserve, aligning with your belief in caring for your skin like Palmolive's gentle promise?

Ask yourself: If you poured both products, in the same color and scent, into identical bowls, would you be able to tell the difference? Maybe, but probably not.

When comparing two otherwise identical products, a strong brand guides customers to choose one product over another. Customers who purchase Palmolive might feel they are prioritizing self-care by choosing a gentle option. On the other hand, Dawn customers may believe they are doing something positive for the environment. Whether or not these brand claims are completely true, it often doesn't matter—what matters is the lasting emotional connection these messages create in your memory, ultimately guiding purchase decisions and brand loyalty. When brands strategically influence emotions, they can encourage repeat purchases and build lasting loyalty.

All these parts, together, create the brand's foundation and distinguish it from other companies. It makes customers want to choose this brand over others. When a brand has a good foundation, it can grow and become more valuable over time. This is why building a strong brand foundation is so critical for companies.

Core components of a brand: The BRAND approach

In the previous section, we saw how one way to think about a brand is that it's like a promise. When customers witness a brand, they expect something. This could be good quality, low prices, or friendly service.

We also saw how every brand has a personality, which refers to how it makes people feel. This is another way to understand brands—to think about feelings. Brands can make people feel happy, excited, or safe. For example, when people see a sports brand, they might feel energetic. When they see a luxury brand, they might feel special.

DISCUSSION Think of a brand that has built a strong emotional connection with you. What specific elements contributed to that connection? Would you call yourself a loyal advocate of this brand, and if so, why?

These foundations of "promises and feelings" contribute to people's overall impression of a company or product. In addition to these two factors, there are other elements that work together to form a brand's impression. We can use the word BRAND as an acronym to help remember these important parts of a brand. Each letter represents a key component contributing to the brand's identity and how people perceive it.

B - Basics: The brand name, logo, and tagline

R - Representation: How the brand looks, like its colors and design

A - Audience: The people the brand wants to reach

N - Narrative: The brand's story and personality

D - Deliverables: What the brand offers and promises

These parts all help make a brand special. They shape how people see and feel about the brand.

1.2 Key Concepts: Brand Awareness, Identity, and Reputation

When we discuss brands, we must know three key concepts: brand awareness, brand identity, and brand reputation. These concepts help us understand how people see and think about brands. They are like building blocks that make a brand strong. Let's look at each one of them to understand why they are important and how they work.

1.2.1 Brand awareness

Brand awareness is about how many people know about a brand. It's like when you play a game and try to remember names. The more you hear a name, the easier it is to remember.

For example, think about soft drinks. You have almost certainly heard of Coca-Cola; most people have. Even if someone doesn't drink this beverage often, when they want a drink, they might think of Coca-Cola first. This is because Coca-Cola has high brand awareness. They use ads, put their logo in many places, and sponsor large events. All these activities help people remember the brand.

Companies can make more people aware of their brand by:

- Putting ads on TV, radio, and the internet
- Using social media to talk to people
- Putting their name on sports teams' t-shirts
- Making their products easy to see in stores

When more people know about a brand, it can help the company sell more. People often buy things they know about, even if there are other choices.

1.2.2 Brand identity

Brand identity is how a brand looks and acts. It's like how a person dresses and talks. A brand's identity helps people recognize it easily.

Again, let's consider Apple, a company known for its consumer electronics and software services. When you see a graphic of an apple with a bite taken out, you are likely to immediately recognize it as Apple's logo. Its logo is iconic and sleek. These qualities extend well beyond the logo and are present in every aspect of Apple's brand. The minimalist and memorable design is exhibited in products like the iPhone and MacBook, as well as their in-store experience, which is intentionally designed to be open and uncluttered.

> **TIP** Consistency in visual style builds trust—think of how Apple uses the same minimalist design across all products.

Even in its marketing, Apple uses direct and accessible language to convey its message. Whether it's the design of their devices or the seamless experience across all points of contact, Apple's branding remains consistent. This makes them one of the most recognizable and trusted brands in the world.

Brand identity includes:

- The brand's logo (like Nike's swoosh)
- Colors the brand uses (like McDonald's red and yellow)
- How the brand's products look
- The words the brand uses in ads
- What the brand believes in

A strong brand identity helps people remember the brand and know what it stands for. It makes the brand different from other brands.

1.2.3 Brand reputation

Brand reputation is what people think about a brand. It's like when people talk about someone they know. They might say the person is nice, smart, or untrustworthy. Brands have reputations, too. For example, Volvo cars have a reputation for being safe. When people think about buying a safe car, they often think of Volvo. This reputation comes from years of making safe cars and telling people about it.

A brand's reputation can come from:

- How good their products are
- How they treat customers
- What do they do to help people or the environment
- What people say about the brand to friends or on online platforms

A good reputation is a crucial component. It can make people want to buy from the brand time and again and tell their friends good things about it.

The components discussed in this section—awareness, identity, and reputation—all work together. A brand needs people to know about it (awareness), recognize it (identity), and think good things about it (reputation). When all these things work well together, a brand can be very successful.

For example, the American athletic footwear and apparel brand Nike is known by many people (high awareness). They recognize the swoosh logo and "Just Do It" slogan (strong identity). Many people think Nike makes good sports shoes and clothes (good reputation). All these things combined help make Nike a strong brand.

These components are essential for brand managers. They help managers make good choices about building and nurturing the brands. For example, if a brand manager knows their brand's identity well, they can create ads that fit that identity. If they understand brand awareness, they can find better ways to tell more people about the brand. If they know about brand reputation, they can work on enhancing people's perception of the brand.

Brand managers who effectively implement these components can help companies scale their brand presence.

They also help customers discover why they like some brands more than others.

In the upcoming section, we will understand the roles of a brand manager in further detail, along with goal-setting for brand managers.

1.3 Becoming a BRAND MASTER

You can think of someone who manages a brand as a BRAND MASTER. A brand master takes on many important tasks to build and protect a brand. They work on different parts of the brand to keep it strong and help it grow.

The BRAND MASTER approach covers the key roles a brand manager plays, as outlined below:

- **B** - Build brand strategy
- **R** - Research market trends
- **A** - Analyze competitor activities
- **N** - Nurture brand identity
- **D** - Develop marketing campaigns

- **M** - Manage brand performance
- **A** - Align with company goals
- **S** - Supervise product development
- **T** - Track consumer insights
- **E** - Ensure brand consistency
- **R** - Report on brand metrics

Effective brand managers understand that adaptability is key to strengthening a brand. The BRAND MASTER approach provides a framework to guide managers throughout a brand's lifecycle. This ensures that the brand offers value and evolves with market changes.

The role of a brand manager is to provide strategic guidance for a brand at all stages of its life, from infancy to maturity. As a brand evolves, the priorities of a brand manager must evolve with it. For example, in the early stages of brand management, the primary focus is on establishing an identity and building awareness. Later, building loyalty and maintaining relevance become more important.

DISCUSSION

As a brand manager, how would you ensure that your brand's foundation aligns with the overall business goals?

The continuous processes of analyzing and positioning brand value and delivering the brand promise are significant in maximizing its impact. These functions are essential to the managers' role in keeping their brand strong and relevant.

Figure 1.1 The role of a brand manager throughout the brand life cycle

Analyze

Plan

Maximize Brand Value

Deliver

Position

1.3.1 Goal-setting for brand managers

Effective planning and goal-setting are important for brand managers as they simplify decision-making by providing a roadmap for actions. Team collaboration is enhanced when everyone is aware of the established plan. Moreover, a clear strategy allows managers to prioritize key aspects that drive the brand's success.

Leading a brand's management plan is like planning for a long trip. Brand managers must know where they want the brand to go and how to get there. Without a defined plan, resources become less efficient, and assessing the brand's performance becomes difficult.

Brand managers develop strategies tailored to their specific objectives, which can vary depending on their primary focus. For instance, if the goal is to enhance brand awareness, the strategy might emphasize marketing and communication efforts. Expanding into new markets might be the approach of choice if the objective is to increase profitability. When targeting new customers, the strategy could center around introducing innovative products that capture their attention. Each of these strategies is uniquely implemented to achieve a specific outcome. Ultimately, it contributes to a brand's strength and long-term success.

In the upcoming section, we'll examine the different ways in which brand managers set goals and make decisions. We'll see how they set clear targets and work towards them. And how these plans fit into the bigger picture for the company. This will help us understand why brand management requires careful thinking and strategy.

1.3.2 Types of brand management goals

Brand managers set different types of goals to guide their work. These goals help them focus on what's most important for the brand. Here are the primary types of goals brand managers often use:

Brand awareness goals

These goals are about increasing the brand's awareness. For example, a goal might be to increase the number of people who recognize the brand name. Brand managers might use more advertising or social media campaigns to reach this goal.

Customer acquisition goals

These goals focus on attracting new customers. A brand manager might set a goal to increase the number of first-time buyers by a certain percentage. They might create new products or offer special deals to attract new customers.

Revenue growth goals

These goals are about making more money for the company. An example of this goal could be to increase sales by a certain amount. Brand managers might try selling in new places or raising prices to meet these goals.

Brand strength goals

These goals aim to strengthen the overall brand. This could include improving how people feel about the brand or making the brand more valuable. Brand managers might work on enhancing product quality or customer service to achieve these goals.

Market expansion goals

These goals relate to growing the brand in new areas or with new groups of customers. Here, the goal might be to enter a new country or appeal to a different age group. Brand managers could create new products or change marketing strategies to reach these goals.

Brand loyalty goals

These goals focus on retaining current customers and making them loyal to the brand. One goal might be increasing repeat purchases. Brand managers might create loyalty programs or improve customer experiences to achieve this goal.

Brand identity goals

These goals are about making the brand's personality and values clear to customers. For example, a goal could be to make customers see the brand as more innovative or eco-friendly. Brand managers might change packaging or start new marketing campaigns to achieve these goals.

Each type of goal requires different strategies and plans. Brand managers often work on several of these goals at the same time. They choose the most important goals based on what the brand needs most. By setting and working towards these goals, they help the brand become stronger and more successful over time.

1.3.3 SMART goals

After understanding the different types of brand management goals, it's important to know how to set them in a way that is clear and achievable. Brand managers often use SMART goals, which ensure that goals are well-defined and can be measured.

S - Specific

The goal should be clear and precise. Instead of "increase brand awareness," a specific goal might be to "increase brand recognition among 18-25-year-olds in the city."

M - Measurable

There should be a way to measure if the goal has been reached. For example, "increase social media followers by 20%" is measurable.

A - Achievable

The goal should be something that can be achieved with the available resources. For a new brand, setting a goal to become the market leader in one month might not be achievable.

R - Relevant

The goal should matter to the brand and fit with its overall plans. A luxury brand probably wouldn't set a goal to be the cheapest option in the market.

T - Time-bound

There should be a clear timeframe for reaching the goal. For instance, "launch a new product line by the end of Q3" gives a specific deadline.

Using SMART goals helps brand managers in several ways:

1. It clarifies goals so everyone on the team understands what needs to be done.
2. It helps in planning because the goals are specific and have deadlines.
3. It makes it easier to see if goals have been achieved because they can be measured.
4. It keeps the team focused on what's most important for the brand.

For example, instead of a general goal like "improve brand awareness," a SMART goal might be to "Increase brand recognition among women aged 25-40 in the Northeast region by 15% within the next six months through targeted social media campaigns and local events."

By using SMART goals, brand managers can make their plans more effective and increase the chances of success for their brand strategies.

1.3.4 Aligning brand goals with business objectives

Brand managers must ensure that their goals align with the company's overall objectives. This strategic alignment is crucial. It ensures that the brand supports the company's broader plans and contributes to its success. Aligning goals also ensures everyone in the company is working towards the same goal. It promotes efficient resource use and demonstrates how the brand directly contributes to the company's success.

To achieve strategic alignment between brand goals and business objectives, brand managers should follow these key steps:

1. **Understand:** Understand the company's overall strategy and objectives clearly.

2. **Communicate:** Regularly engage with other departments to ensure brand goals support company-wide initiatives.

3. **Measure:** Use metrics that are relevant to both brand performance and overall business success.

4. **Relate:** Ensure each brand goal directly contributes to at least one business objective.

5. **Adapt:** Be prepared to adjust brand goals as business objectives evolve.

6. **Report:** Consistently demonstrate how brand performance impacts business results.

For example, if a company's overall goal is to increase market share by 5% in the next year, a brand manager might set these aligned goals:

- Increase brand awareness by 15% among the target demographic through a multi-channel marketing campaign.

- Improve customer retention rate by 10% by enhancing the brand's loyalty program.

- Launch two new product lines that address unmet needs in the market, aiming to capture new customer segments.

By setting these brand-specific goals, the brand manager directly contributes to the company's objective of increasing market share. The awareness campaign attracts new customers, the improved loyalty program retains existing ones, and the new product lines help capture additional market segments. This alignment ensures that brand management efforts are not just building the brand but also actively driving the company's growth and success.

In the next section, we will look at the journey of a brand. Understanding the stages of a brand's journey helps brand managers make better plans and guide their brands to success.

1.4 The Journey of a Brand - From Awareness to Loyalty

Brands grow and change over time. Their journeys begin when people first hear about them and can go on to customers who love the brand and keep buying from it. A brand's journey has different steps, each important in building a strong, successful brand. As shown in Figure 1.2 below, this journey from awareness to loyalty follows a series of stages that are key to establishing long-term success.

Figure 1.2 The brand journey

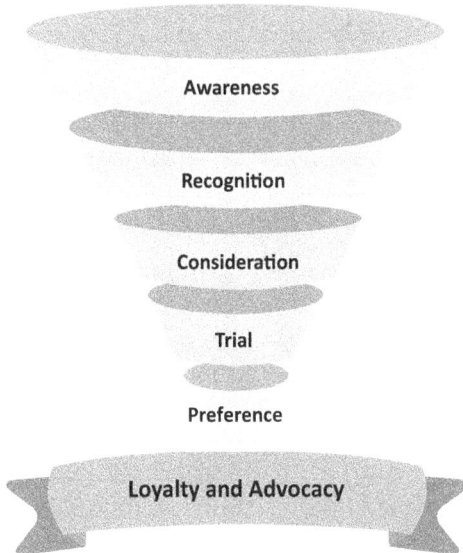

Brand awareness

This is when people first learn about a brand. They might see an ad or hear about it from friends. People know the brand exists at this stage, but don't know much about it. Brand managers work hard to make more people aware of the brand. They might use television ads, social media, or special events to tell people about the brand.

Brand recognition

After awareness comes recognition. This is when people can identify the brand when they see it. They might recognize the logo or remember the brand name. Brand managers focus on making the brand easy to remember. They use consistent colors, logos, and messages to help people recognize the brand quickly.

Brand consideration

At this stage, people think about buying from the brand. They compare it to other brands they know. They might discuss quality, price, or special features that differentiate the brand. Brand managers try to show why their brand is better than others.

Brand trial

This is when people try the brand for the first time. It's a very important step. Brand managers want to ensure a good first experience. They might offer free samples or special deals to encourage people to try the brand.

Brand preference

If people like their experience with the brand, they might start to prefer it over other brands. They begin to choose this brand more often when they shop. Brand managers work on keeping the quality high and making customers happy to build this preference.

Brand loyalty and advocacy

This is the final stage of the journey. Loyal customers love the brand and keep buying from it. They might even tell their friends about it. Brand managers focus on keeping these customers happy. They might have special programs for loyal customers or ask for their opinions on new products.

Throughout this journey, brand managers use different strategies to move customers from one stage to the next. They make sure the brand keeps its promises at every stage. They listen to what customers say and make changes if needed, trying to build emotional connections with customers. They keep the brand's message clear and consistent and use the brand values to guide all their decisions.

Brand managers use different strategies to help customers move from one stage to the next in their brand journey. Table 1.1 outlines examples of strategies used at various stages of the brand journey.

Table 1.1	Moving customers through the brand journey
Brand awareness	• Use ads on TV, social media, and other places people often see • Work with famous people or experts to talk about the brand • Be part of community events or support good causes
Brand recognition	• Make sure the brand looks the same everywhere (like using the same colors and logo) • Tell stories about the brand that people will remember • Put the brand name or logo in places where people will see it a lot
Brand consideration	• Show how the brand is different from others • Give people useful information about the product or service • Let people try the product for free or at a lower price
Brand trial	• Make it easy for people to buy or try the product • Offer good deals for first-time buyers • Make sure the first experience with the brand is really good
Brand preference	• Keep making good products or services • Listen to what customers say and make things better • Give special treatment to people who buy often
Brand loyalty	• Start a program that gives rewards to loyal customers • Ask loyal customers what they think and use their ideas • Make customers feel like they're part of a special group

Not all customers will become loyal. Some might stay at the awareness or recognition stage. However, brand managers always try to move people towards loyalty. They know that loyal customers are very valuable to the brand.

As brands go through this journey, they often become more than just products. They can become part of people's lives and identities. This is why brand management is so important. It helps create strong brands that people love and trust. By understanding this journey, brand managers can make better plans. This helps strengthen the brand over time.

1.4.1 Measuring brand loyalty and engagement

Brand managers who excel at creating strategies and aligning them with business objectives must also be skilled in measuring the effectiveness of their work. Understanding how to measure brand loyalty and engagement is crucial for success. Even the best strategies can fall short of their potential without proper measurement.

Key Performance Indicators (KPIs) are essential tools for brand managers. KPIs are specific, measurable values that show how well a brand achieves its goals. They help track progress and ensure informed decision-making. They demonstrate the value of brand strategies to company leadership.

Brand loyalty and engagement can be observed through various customer behaviors and attitudes. For example, repeat purchases and positive word-of-mouth indicate a strong connection to the brand. Actively participating in the brand's community through mediums such as online forums or social media is also a sign of loyalty because it shows that customers are willing to invest their time and energy to support and engage with a brand.

While we will explore specific measurement techniques later in Chapter 8, brand managers should know that quantitative (numerical) and qualitative (descriptive) data play essential roles in understanding brand loyalty and engagement. Analyzing sales data, conducting customer surveys, monitoring social media interactions, and gathering feedback through focus groups or interviews are some methods to measure brand loyalty and engagement.

1.4.2 Purpose-driven branding

We've seen how brands grow and change over time. Now, let's look at a special way of building brands called purpose-driven branding, which is becoming increasingly important in today's world.

Purpose-driven branding means a brand does more than just sell things. It's when a brand has a clear reason for existing beyond making money. This reason shapes how the brand acts and what it offers to customers. It shows that good brand management means creating a brand that means something to people and has a bigger goal to help people or improve the world. This goal guides everything the brand does.

A brand's purpose should be:

- Real and honest
- Connected to what the brand does
- Something the brand can help with
- Easy to understand

Purpose-driven branding is important for many reasons. It is part of the brand's identity, and it helps brands connect with customers who care about the same things. Thus, it makes the brand easy to remember. It can also help more people know about the brand. Purpose-driven branding can help move customers from just knowing about the brand to really liking it. When customers feel a brand cares about important issues, they often become more loyal.

The brand's purpose helps managers make decisions about products and marketing. Brand managers can use it as part of their plans to make the brand stronger. Thinking about a bigger purpose can also lead to new ideas for products or ways of doing business. Ultimately, it leads to a stronger brand.

Purpose-driven branding integrates all elements of a business, including its offering, culture, strategy, people, communication, and operations, to align with a central purpose and create consistent value. This is exhibited in Figure 1.3 below:

Figure 1.3 Purpose-driven brand framework

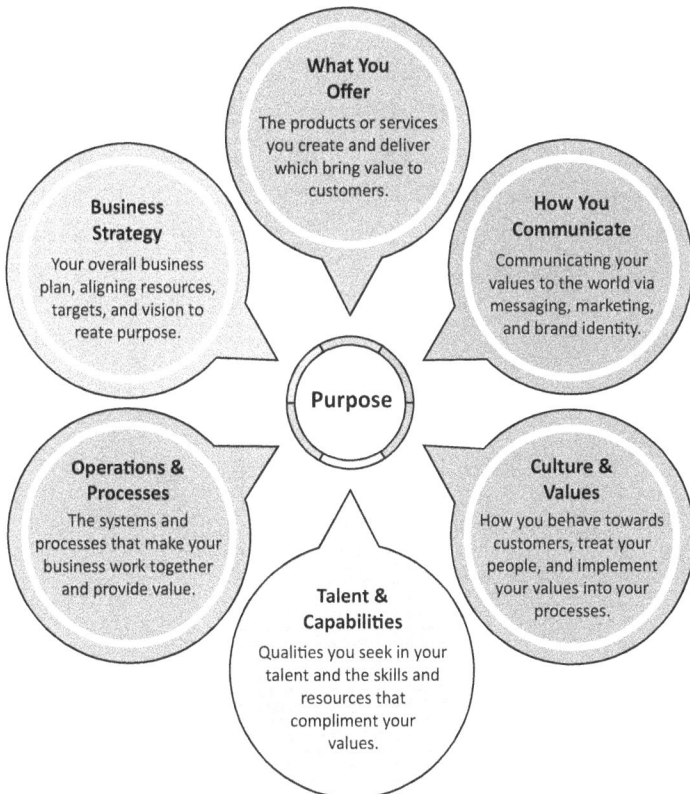

Purpose-driven branding connects with customers by conveying values that go beyond profit.

As we conclude Chapter 1, you now have a clear understanding of the fundamental building blocks of a brand and how they guide customers along a journey from recognition to loyalty. You've also explored the brand manager's core responsibilities and the impact of purpose-driven branding in building stronger connections. These insights lay a solid foundation for effective brand management and set the stage for your next steps.

In the next chapter, you'll learn how to identify and segment your target audience. By combining the foundational concepts you've learned with data-driven audience insights, you'll have the tools to create focused strategies that resonate with the right people and drive long-term brand success.

Chapter Summary

- Brand: What people think and feel about a company or product, including its name, logo, and reputation.

- Core brand components include the name, logo, tagline, visual identity, personality, promise, target audience, values, and offerings.

- Brand awareness is about how many people know about the brand.

- Brand identity refers to how the brand looks and acts.

- Brand Reputation refers to what people think about the brand based on quality and customer service.

- Brand management helps create and maintain a strong brand image to stand out.

- Brand managers develop strategies, research trends, analyze competitors, nurture brand identity, and create marketing campaigns.

- SMART goals are Specific, Measurable, Achievable, Relevant, and Time-bound objectives for guiding brand managers.

- Aligning brand goals with business objectives ensures that brand activities support the company's overall plans.

- The brand journey moves from awareness to recognition, consideration, trial, preference, and loyalty.

- Purpose-driven branding means having a bigger goal beyond making money, like helping people or the environment.

- Measuring brand loyalty and engagement involves using Key Performance Indicators (KPIs) to track success.

- Building emotional connections with customers leads to loyalty and long-term success.

- Effective brand management helps companies adapt to market changes while staying true to their identity.

Quiz

1. **What is a brand, according to David Ogilvy?**
   a. Just a logo and name
   b. A product's price and packaging
   c. The intangible sum of a product's attributes
   d. A company's advertising strategy

2. **Which of the following is NOT a core component of a brand?**
   a. Brand name
   b. Logo
   c. Financial statements
   d. Brand personality

3. **What do the "R"s in the BRAND MASTER approach stand for?**
   a. Revise marketing strategies & Report brand metrics
   b. Research market trends & Report brand metrics
   c. Review customer feedback & Refine product features
   d. Reallocate budgets & Renew brand identity

4. **Which stage in the brand journey comes immediately after brand awareness?**
   a. Brand loyalty
   b. Brand preference
   c. Brand recognition
   d. Brand consideration

5. **What is the primary goal of brand management?**
   a. To create catchy slogans
   b. To increase short-term sales
   c. To reduce marketing costs
   d. To create and maintain a strong brand image

6. **Which of the following best describes purpose-driven branding?**
   a. Focusing solely on profit maximization
   b. Having a goal that helps people or makes the world better
   c. Creating the most expensive products in the market
   d. Changing the brand's logo frequently

7. **What is brand identity?**
   a. How many people know about the brand
   b. The financial value of the brand
   c. How the brand looks and acts
   d. The number of loyal customers

8. **Which of the following is the responsibility of a brand manager?**
   a. Manufacturing products
   b. Hiring employees
   c. Developing marketing campaigns
   d. Setting product prices

9. How does effective brand management contribute to long-term success?
   a. By focusing only on short-term sales
   b. By changing the brand's core identity frequently
   c. By adapting to market changes while maintaining core identity
   d. By ignoring customer feedback

10. What is the difference between brand awareness and brand recognition?
    a. They are the same thing.
    b. Brand awareness is knowing the brand exists; recognition is identifying it when seen.
    c. Brand recognition comes before brand awareness.
    d. Brand awareness is only about the logo; recognition is about the product.

Answers

1 – c	2 – c	3 – b	4 – c	5 – d
6 – b	7 – c	8 – c	9 – c	10 – b

CHAPTER 2

Knowing Your Customer

Key Learning Objectives

- Understand why pinpointing a target audience is crucial for brand success.
- Learn how to split audiences using factors like demographics, psychology, behavior, and location.
- Find out how to build thorough customer personas by examining challenges, goals, and desires.
- Explore how to align your brand with customer expectations through gap analysis and value statements.

Brand success begins with knowing who you serve. This chapter shows how to spot and group your audience, form detailed personas, and match your brand to what customers want.

You'll see how brand managers study customer struggles, goals, and desires to shape better experiences. We'll also explore ways to use segmentation methods, data insights, and personalization to build lasting customer connections.

2.1 Defining and Segmenting Your Target Audience

In Chapter 1, you saw that a brand manager's job includes keeping the brand relevant for the long term. This requires knowing exactly who you want to reach. Without this clarity, your messages may be too broad and won't engage the right people.

This section defines a target audience and explains how to segment it. You'll also explore methods that brand managers use to find the right audience. Using these ideas, you can refine your message and better connect with the people who matter most.

2.1.1 Target audiences

A brand's target audience is a group of consumers with shared qualities who are most likely to connect with a brand.

These individuals have similar needs, preferences, or expectations. Recognizing these similarities helps a brand manager create messages that truly resonate with consumers. This focus also ensures that resources go toward the people most interested in the brand instead of casting too wide a net.

Consider NatureBoots, a fictional brand that sells premium hiking boots. Its brand manager targets hiking enthusiasts who need sturdy gear for rough terrain. In this case, the manager tailors messaging, distribution, and product features to meet the specific needs of these customers rather than appealing to every footwear shopper in the broad market.

The broad market is the entire group of consumers in a market; a target audience is a group of consumers who are aligned with a brand's offering.

Figure 2.1 Target audience vs. Broad market

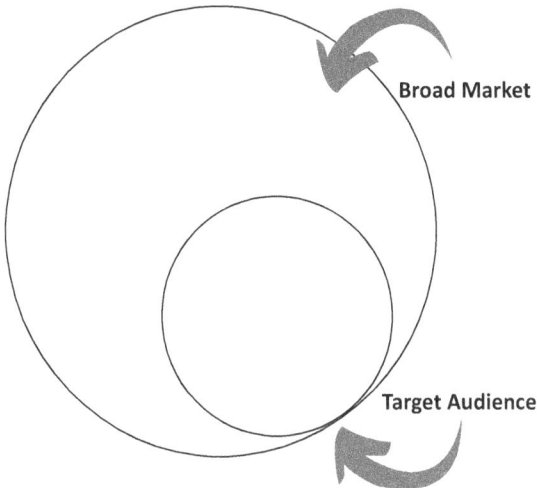

Broad Market

Target Audience

2.1.2 Audience segmentation

Once a target audience is defined, it's important to realize that this group isn't all the same. Their needs and behaviors can vary widely. This is where audience segmentation becomes essential.

Audience segmentation refers to breaking down the larger, defined target audience and sorting (segmenting) it into smaller, even more specific subgroups based on shared traits. Brand managers need to segment their target audience because doing so provides an increasingly narrowed-in and detailed view of who they are directing their brand outputs to.

Since different subgroups of a target audience will inevitably have different reasons for interacting with a brand, it is logical that there should be unique messages and brand offerings designed for each subgroup. This ensures the brand most closely appeals to their specific needs in each situation.

The target audience at NatureBoots was defined as hiking enthusiasts who buy premium hiking boots suitable for challenging terrain. However, with an urge to understand this group on a deeper level, NatureBoots' brand manager found that this target audience indeed consisted of smaller subgroups who shared similar needs. The manager found that this group of hiking enthusiasts fell into one of the following three segments:

1. Young, affluent social media influencers
2. Seasoned hiking enthusiasts and long-time trekkers
3. Safety-conscious hikers encountering difficult terrain frequently

Despite all three subgroups falling into the same target audience of hiking enthusiasts in the premium hiking boot market, they have different characteristics and needs. These differences should be catered to separately through brand messages, product features, and communication channels.

A brand manager who can understand and acknowledge these differences will be able to create deeper meaning for the members of each segment. This will ultimately lead to stronger connections and consistent relevance, which are key to a successful brand strategy.

FUN FACT
In Japan, KitKat is available in over 300 flavors! This extreme segmentation shows how brands tailor offerings to local tastes.

Segmenting a target audience involves establishing shared interests and characteristics among members to create subgroups of similar audience members. In Figure 2.2 below, the target audience on the left-hand side of the graphic has been segmented into three distinct subgroups based on shared commonalities.

Figure 2.2 Segments of a target audience

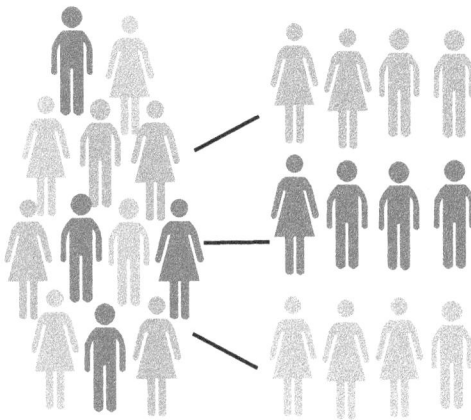

2.1.3 Four dimensions of segmentation

Segmenting an audience involves analyzing it through various lenses, or dimensions, to uncover shared traits and preferences that can guide brand strategy. While these dimensions often overlap, understanding each one individually helps brand managers form a more detailed and actionable profile of the audience. The most common dimensions of segmentation are demographic, psychographic, behavioral, and geographic.

Table 2.1	Four dimensions of segmentation

Dimension	Definition	Examples
Demographic	Groups based on measurable, factual characteristics	Age, gender, income, education, occupation
Psychographic	Groups based on lifestyle, values, and personality traits	Values, attitudes, interests, personality traits
Behavioral	Groups based on observed actions and habits	Purchase frequency, loyalty, product usage habits, online engagement
Geographic	Groups based on physical location or environment	Region, climate, urban vs. rural setting, country-specific cultural preferences

Source: Adapted from Kotler and Keller, 2016.

By combining insights from demographic, psychographic, behavioral, and geographic dimensions, brand managers gain a well-rounded understanding of their customers and create audience segments to best connect with them.

> **TIP** Using quick social media polls or surveys can help brand managers gather real-time customer feedback for effective segmentation.

When the brand manager at NatureBoots set out to segment their audience, they started with the broad target audience of hiking enthusiasts who buy premium hiking boots. By analyzing this audience through the four dimensions of segmentation, they identified three key segments mentioned below, each of which shares similar characteristics:

1. **Young, affluent social media influencers:**

   A. Demographic:

   - Primarily 20-35 years old, with disposable income.
   - Most often, they are single or without children.

   B. Psychographic:

   - Self-image is of great importance, motivated by trends.
   - Value aesthetics and align purchases with their personal brand in mind.

   C. Behavioral:

   - Frequently post their hiking experiences on social media and tag brands.
   - Look for products that enhance their perceived expertise or lifestyle.

   D. Geographic:

   - They live in urban areas but travel to popular outdoor destinations.

2. **Seasoned hiking enthusiasts and long-time trekkers:**

   A. Demographic:

   - Middle-aged (35-55), with a steady income.
   - Preference for practical, reliable footwear.

   B. Psychographic:

   - Knowledgeable about hiking and outdoor gear.
   - Prioritize functionality and durability over style.

- Value a strong connection to nature and see hiking as part of their identity.

C. Behavioral

- Tendency to make purchases based on product reviews or recommendations from trusted sources.

D. Geographic

- They live near outdoor trails, suburban, or rural areas.

3. **Safety-conscious hikers encountering difficult terrain frequently:**

A. Demographic:

- A mix of experienced and intermediate hikers, aged 25-45.
- Varying levels of disposable income.

B. Psychographic:

- Goal-oriented risk takers.
- Value safety and confidence during their hikes, particularly in challenging or unpredictable environments.

C. Behavioral:

- Conduct extensive research before purchasing.
- Often known to look for certifications or technical features like "water resistance" and "superior grip."

D. Geographic

- Commonly live near or frequently travel to mountainous regions

> **POINT TO REMEMBER** Effective segmentation divides a broad audience into specific groups based on demographics, psychographics, behavior, and geography.

This example demonstrates how, despite all the above categories falling into the target audience for premium hiking boots, each segment requires brand messaging tailored to their unique priorities. In this example, a product that communicates having a strong grip and water resistance will resonate well with "safety-conscious hikers" but will likely be of little value to "social media influencers." Thus, understanding the differences between segments allows the brand manager at NatureBoots to create strategies tailored to each segment, contributing to better brand connections and overall success.

2.1.4 How to segment an audience

To effectively segment a target audience, brand managers rely on the collection and analysis of data that truly provides an understanding of who their target audience is. It is important to ensure that data is both reliable and relevant to ensure segmentation is based on facts instead of guesswork. Data can be gathered from a variety of sources that relate to your target audience. Common sources that brand managers use for segmentation are:

1. **Surveys and questionnaires:** Direct insights from large groups of customers to provide data relating to preferences, behaviors, and expectations.

2. **Interviews and focus groups:** Narrowed insights from smaller groups provide data about motivations and challenges.

3. **Social listening and online analytics:** Monitoring social media platforms, chat forums, and review sites to understand what customers are saying provides helpful segmentation data in real-time settings.

4. **Sales data:** Historical data can provide segmentation insights based on long-term trends and customer purchase behaviors.

5. **Customer Relationship Management (CRM) systems:** CRM systems provide useful data on customer journeys and brand loyalty.

Once a brand manager has collected a sufficient amount of data, they will be able to identify trends or patterns that define the subgroups within a target audience. This is accomplished by seeking out shared characteristics that fall into the four dimensions of segmentation. These shared characteristics can then be used to tell a story about the segment of customers, and this story can be used to inform the brand strategy for that segment.

Identifying a target audience and using segmentation tools to break that audience into meaningful groups is a key step in brand management. The four dimensions of segmentation—demographic, psychographic, behavioral, and geographic allow brand managers to paint a clearer picture of their customers. Data-driven segmentation based on careful analysis ensures those segments are both accurate and actionable. With a well-defined target audience in place, a brand manager can create more relevant brand experiences that resonate with customers and, therefore, drive loyalty, growth, and sustain brand value.

2.2 Customer Personas – Pain Points, Aspirations, and Motivations

After identifying a target audience and creating audience segments, the next step is creating detailed customer personas. It's not enough to know who your customers are; you need to understand why they make their choices. This deeper knowledge makes your engagement more meaningful.

To gain this knowledge, you need to examine customers' key attributes, pain points, aspirations, and motivations. Such insights enable brand managers to build messages and products that truly connect with customers.

2.2.1 Building a customer persona

A customer persona is a semi-fictional representation of an ideal customer segment based on real market research and data (Kotler & Keller, 2016).

A persona typically covers demographics, psychographics, values, buying habits, and emotional triggers like pain points or aspirations. These details reveal why customers act as they do, helping brand managers connect with them more effectively.

2.2.2 Customer pain points

This includes specific problems, frustrations, or unmet needs that customers experience in their daily lives or when interacting with certain products or services (Goodwin, 2009).

Understanding customer pain points allows brand managers to create solutions that directly address problems or frustrations experienced by customers. Positioning a brand as a solution to a customer problem helps to deepen brand relevance and appeal.

While customer pain points can be known or obvious issues faced by customers that cause frustrations, they can also be more hidden in the sense of unmet needs. In the second case, customers might not always be aware of a pain point. Brand managers, therefore, have an opportunity not only to address known customer frustrations but also to identify unmet needs. By doing so, they can deliver solutions to problems customers didn't even realize they had.

Brand managers should stay on top of industry news and trends to ensure they can act quickly when a customer pain point is identified. Common methods of identifying pain points include direct feedback from customers, social listening, and customer support interactions.

A brand manager can be reactive in responding to pain points that customers are experiencing from their brand, or they can be proactive in providing solutions to pain points experienced by customers interacting outside of their brand.

2.2.3 Customer aspirations

Beyond solving problems, brand managers should also understand what customers aspire to achieve—be it growth, convenience, social recognition, or simply more enjoyment in their free time. This understanding can help the brand manager position the brand offering as a solution to fulfilling a customer's aspirations.

Customer aspirations refer to the desired outcomes, lifestyles, or statuses that individuals hope to attain, often through the products and services they choose (Kotler & Keller, 2016).

It is rare for customers to make purchases based on a single reason. Instead, customers are generally motivated by a combination of functional needs, emotional desires, and social factors. Understanding these decision drivers can help brand managers frame their value proposition in a way that appeals directly to what customers care about most.

For example, a fitness apparel company might discover that its customers value community support just as much as the product itself. Therefore, highlighting membership in a supportive, like-minded community could play a key role in the brand's messaging.

2.2.4 Creating customer personas for brand strategy

As seen at the beginning of Section 2.2, the personification of segments is useful for determining messaging and brand offerings. Personas are used as practical tools for guiding brand decisions because they influence everything from marketing campaigns and communication tone to product features and customer service approaches.

By analyzing pain points, aspirations, and motivations, you can develop actionable personas. An actionable persona is a semi-fictional profile that guides decision-making in brand management.

Each persona should represent a distinct segment with its own needs and behaviors. Overlapping personas can cause confusion and harm brand strategy, as it's unclear which group you're truly serving. Clear distinctions let brand managers tailor approaches to specific pain points and desires, ensuring that messaging and offerings resonate more deeply.

> **POINT TO REMEMBER**
> Customer personas provide detailed insights into the unique needs, pain points, and aspirations of different audience segments.

Brand managers can use the customer persona template in Figure 2.3 below to create fictional characters that reflect a customer persona. This tool helps identify key traits, goals, and motivations, enabling brand managers to make informed decisions on how to engage each segment.

Figure 2.3 Customer persona template

CUSTOMER PERSONA #1		
	INTERESTS	
	CHALLENGES	
	HOW CAN WE FIX THEIR CHALLENGES?	
	GOALS	
NAME	MOTIVATION	
AGE		
LOCATION	PAIN POINTS/FRUSTRATIONS	
OCCUPATION		
MARITAL STATUS	SOURCES OF INFO	
KIDS		
ANNUAL INCOME	ADDITIONAL.	

Source: Adapted from Canva

> **DISCUSSION**
> What are the characteristics you would include in a customer persona for your favorite brand, and why?

2.3 Matching Your Brand-to-Customer Expectations

After you know who your customers are and why they buy, the next step is making sure your brand meets their needs. People have standards for product quality, service, and overall experience. Exceeding these standards can transform occasional buyers into loyal, long-term customers.

2.3.1 Understanding customer expectations

Customers have two types of expectations: "explicit" and "implicit." To stay competitive and build loyalty, brand managers should address both.

1. **Explicit:** Clearly stated needs, such as durability or comfort

2. **Implicit:** Assumed requirements, like a warranty or ethical production

For example, when buying premium hiking boots, a customer "explicitly" expects durability, comfort, and water resistance. However, they might "implicitly" assume that the boots come with a reliable warranty or are ethically manufactured.

2.3.2 Aligning a brand with customer expectations

Meeting customer expectations starts with a well-thought-out plan. This plan should aim to identify gaps, refine offerings, and build trust. Below are the four key steps that guide brand managers through this process:

Step 1: Conduct a gap analysis

A gap analysis compares what your brand currently delivers with what customers want. This reveals areas where you might fall short. It provides brand managers with the insight and actions required to solve customer pain points. For instance, if customers expect fast shipping but often face delays, that gap needs attention. By spotting these gaps, you can plan improvements that keep customers satisfied and loyal.

Questions to ask:

- Where might the brand be underperforming, based on feedback?
- Is there something customers expect that competitors provide but you do not?

Figure 2.4 Gap analysis

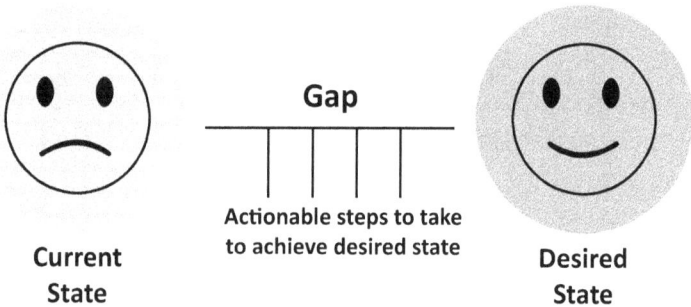

Gap

Actionable steps to take to achieve desired state

Current State

Desired State

Step 2: Refine the value proposition

A value proposition is a clear statement that explains why someone should choose your brand. Focus on how your brand meets audience needs and what unique benefits you offer compared to competitors. This clarity helps each customer segment see why your brand stands out.

Step 3: Deliver on the brand promise

Stay consistent with the experience you promise—whether that is a high performance, excellent service, or something unique. Every touchpoint should reinforce this promise. Customers build trust when they see that your actions match your words.

Step 4: Use customer feedback loops

Collect and analyze feedback regularly through reviews, surveys, and direct interactions. This helps you keep track of changing customer expectations and adjust your strategy as needed. Early insight from feedback loops can also guide improvements before problems escalate.

When a brand consistently meets or exceeds expectations, customers tend to come back and also share their experiences with others, ultimately becoming loyal advocates. This alignment sets the stage for long-term success.

2.4 Personalizing a Brand

In today's fast-paced markets, personalization is no longer optional—it's expected. Customers want to feel recognized and valued. Brands that fail to offer personalized experiences risk being overlooked by those that can.

Personalization means tailoring every interaction—messaging, offers, and engagement—to fit each customer or segment. By using insights from audience segmentation, brand managers can build more personalized connections that lead to higher loyalty. For instance, to reach the young, affluent social media influencers segment at NatureBoots, a brand manager might create exclusive online communities, give early access to new product launches, or highlight lifestyle appeal and aspirational design.

While personalization is crucial, brand managers should keep the brand's integrity intact. A consistent voice and identity foster trust and brand recognition. As you adapt messages and product recommendations to suit different segments, also ensure you stay true to the brand's core values and promises.

Methods of personalization

Brand managers have several tools for creating tailored experiences:

1. **Data-driven customization**

   By using CRM tools, purchase history analysis, and engagement analytics, brand managers can develop strategies to provide personalized product suggestions, discounts, or communication.

2. **Segment-specific messaging**

   Managers can tailor campaigns to specific audience segments based on shared traits, such as interests, location, or purchase behavior.

3. **Dynamic customer journeys**

   Flexible customer journeys that respond to individual interactions can be created to further personalize the brand experience. This could include personalized emails or retargeting ads that are triggered when a customer visits the brand website.

Ethical considerations

With personalization comes the responsibility to handle customer data ethically. Transparency about data collection and usage builds trust. On the other hand, privacy concerns can erode it. Brand managers must ensure that there is full compliance with data protection regulations and communicate their practices clearly to customers.

Future trends

As technology evolves, so will personalization. Artificial intelligence, predictive analytics, and real-time personalization tools will allow brands to anticipate customer needs and deliver highly relevant experiences.

By deeply understanding your audience, segmenting them wisely, aligning your brand with customer expectations, and offering tailored experiences, you build the groundwork for meaningful connections. A clear target audience is just the beginning. Lasting success hinges on a brand manager's ability to adapt, earn trust, and stay relevant in an ever-shifting marketplace. In the upcoming chapter, we'll learn more about the various factors that contribute to building a sustainable and authentic brand.

Chapter Summary

- A target audience is a specific group of consumers most likely to engage with a brand, defined by shared characteristics, needs, or preferences.

- Audience segmentation divides a broad audience into smaller subgroups based on traits such as demographics, psychographics, behavior, and geography.

- Demographic segmentation uses measurable factors like age, gender, and income to group customers.

- Psychographic segmentation examines values, attitudes, and lifestyles to uncover customer motivations and interests.

- Behavioral segmentation focuses on customer actions, such as purchase habits, brand loyalty, and product usage.

- Geographic segmentation analyzes physical location and environmental factors, such as region, climate, or urban versus rural settings.

- Customer personas are detailed profiles combining segmentation insights, providing a comprehensive understanding of ideal customer segments.

- Pain points are customer frustrations or unmet needs that brands can solve to create value and build trust.

- Aspirations reflect the goals or lifestyles customers wish to achieve, which brands can use to align offerings and messaging.

- Matching a brand to customer expectations involves addressing both explicit and implicit expectations to build trust and loyalty.

- A gap analysis helps identify discrepancies between customer expectations and current brand performance, guiding improvement efforts.

- Personalization tailors interactions and offerings to individual customers or audience segments, enhancing engagement and loyalty.

- Consistency in messaging and delivery ensures that personalized experiences align with the brand's core identity and values.

- Ethical personalization respects data privacy and transparency, fostering customer trust while meeting personalization demands.

- Evolving technology, such as AI and predictive analytics, will continue to shape future personalization and audience segmentation efforts.

Quiz

1. **What is a target audience?**
   a. A brand's largest group of customers
   b. A specific group of consumers most likely to engage with a brand
   c. All potential customers worldwide
   d. Individuals who interact with a brand on social media

2. **Why is audience segmentation important for brand managers?**
   a. To create generic campaigns for all customers
   b. To focus on product development exclusively
   c. To tailor messages and offerings for specific subgroups
   d. To eliminate customers outside the target market

3. **Which of the following is NOT a dimension of audience segmentation?**
   a. Behavioral
   b. Geographic
   c. Demographic
   d. Visual

4. **A psychographic segment would likely focus on:**
   a. Age and income levels
   b. Purchase frequency
   c. Personality traits and values
   d. Urban versus rural locations

5. **What method can brand managers use to identify customer pain points?**
   a. Sales quotas
   b. Focus groups and social listening
   c. Product giveaways
   d. Random sampling

6. **Customer pain points can include:**
   a. Product features they already love
   b. Problems or unmet needs they experience
   c. Frequent social media interactions
   d. Recommendations from friends

7. **Which of the following is an example of an explicit customer expectation?**
   a. Assuming a premium product will have excellent warranty coverage
   b. Expecting a product to be durable and water-resistant
   c. Believing a company should be environmentally responsible
   d. Valuing social recognition from brand usage

8. **What is a customer persona?**
   a. A random profile created for marketing purposes
   b. A semi-fictional representation of an ideal customer segment
   c. A direct feedback report from a customer survey
   d. A generic customer profile that applies to all brands

9. Which segmentation method involves analyzing online engagement and purchase behavior?

   a. Geographic
   b. Psychographic
   c. Behavioral
   d. Demographic

10. What does the Gap Analysis method achieve for a brand manager?

    a. It outlines competitors' strategies.
    b. It identifies discrepancies between customer expectations and brand delivery.
    c. It predicts future market trends.
    d. It determines pricing strategies.

Answers

1 – b	2 – c	3 – d	4 – c	5 – b
6 – b	7 – b	8 – b	9 – c	10 – b

CHAPTER 3
Building a Sustainable Brand

Key Learning Objectives

- Understand how the Brand Identity Prism helps create a unified brand personality.
- Learn to develop a Unique Value Proposition (UVP) that makes your brand stand out.
- Explore how logos, colors, and visuals shape customer perceptions and build emotional connections.
- Establish a consistent brand voice and messaging strategy for clear communication.
- Understand how authenticity and integrity foster trust and loyalty.

In Chapter 2, you learned the significance of a brand manager's comprehensive understanding of their customers. To develop this understanding, you learned how to identify and segment your target audience. You identified customer pain points, aspirations, and motivations. The next step is creating a brand that meets their needs. A sustainable brand connects with its audience and stands out in the market. It remains authentic and adapts to evolving trends and needs.

In this chapter, you'll explore how brand managers use customer insights to build a brand. This includes creating a clear identity and highlighting unique values. It also emphasizes integrating visuals and a consistent brand voice. This approach helps develop a brand that is both authentic and sustainable.

3.1 Developing a Brand Identity

When shaping brand identity, managers should create a clear and cohesive personality. This includes how the brand looks externally and the values it reflects internally. A common framework used by brand managers to guide this process is Kapferer's (1992) Brand Identity Prism.

> **FUN FACT**
>
> LEGO refreshes its brand identity every decade while keeping its core values. This ensures it remains both nostalgic and modern.

This prism consists of six interrelated components that collectively contribute to and define a brand's identity. These components are organized in a prism structure, which also considers the interaction between the "Sender" (the brand) and the "Receiver" (the audience), as well as the processes of "Externalization and Internalization."

3.1.1 The Brand Identity Prism Framework

Kapferer's (1992) prism model shows that a brand's identity is shaped by both external and internal factors. Externalization reflects how the brand presents itself to the world. Internalization focuses on how it connects with the audience's self-image. Each part of the prism helps ensure that the brand stays consistent and resonates with customers emotionally.

Figure 3.1 Brand identity prism

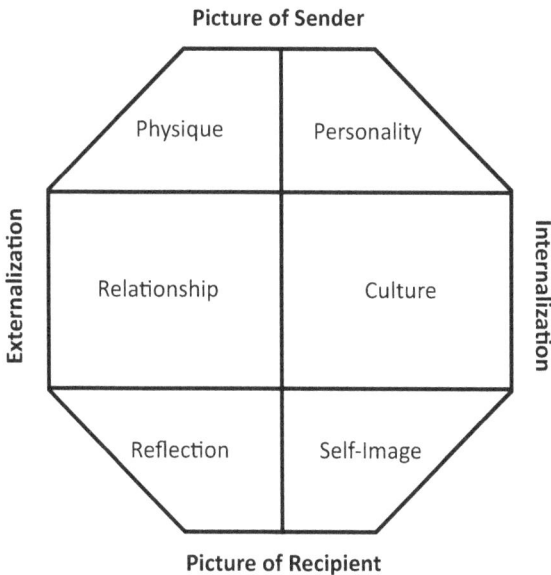

The brand identity prism shows six components of brand identity across two axes: sender/receiver and externalization/internalization (Kapferer, 1992). The six components include: physique, personality, culture, self-image, reflection, and relationship. Each element helps create a brand that customers can recognize, trust, and connect with emotionally. Together, they form and communicate a clear, cohesive identity.

Each of the two main axes or ideas, internalization vs. externalization and sender vs. receiver, around which the prism is organized, has specific meanings. The sender-receiver axis highlights the connection between the brand's identity and how the audience perceives it, ensuring both sides are balanced and aligned.

Using this prism gives brand managers the means to ensure that external messaging is synchronous with internal values and also resonates with their audience. It helps managers maintain consistency across all touchpoints and stand out in the market.

Table 3.1   **Components of the brand identity prism**

Component	Description	Example
Physique (Externalization – Sender)	The tangible and physical elements of the brand, such as logos, packaging, or product design. This component is what is recognizable about the brand, creating an immediate visual impression.	A luxury watch brand could include sleek designs, elegant typography, and a timeless aesthetic.
Personality (Internalization – Sender)	The human traits a brand embodies and its communication approach. This component helps the brand establish a tone of voice and develop emotional engagement with the audience.	A pet food brand might have a caring personality, reinforcing its promise to prioritize your pet's well-being.
Culture (Internalization – Sender)	The core values and principles of the brand. Culture communicates what the company stands for and sets it apart from competitors.	A technology brand could emphasize innovation and boldness, projecting a culture of constant reinvention.

Component	Description	Example
Relationship (Externalization – Receiver)	The connection that the brand builds with its audience. A relationship is the tone and nature of the brand's interactions, for example, professional or collaborative.	A luxury concierge service that fosters a relationship based on exclusivity and personalized attention.
Reflection (Externalization – Receiver)	How the brand sees its ideal customer. This image differs from self-image and reflects the brand's external expression to its audience.	A craft beer company might reflect an image of laid-back individuals who value authenticity and craftsmanship.
Self-Image (Internalization – Receiver)	How customers perceive themselves when interacting with the brand. This component aligns the brand's identity with the audience's desired identity or sense of self.	A premium fitness apparel brand might appeal to customers who view themselves as disciplined and health-conscious.

Source: Kapferer's Brand Identity Prism (Kapferer, 1992)

3.1.2 Applying the Brand Identity Prism

The brand identity prism framework allows brand managers to get a holistic view of their brand. Each component of the prism should align to form a consistent identity that resonates with customers. This alignment also helps a brand stand out from competitors in the market.

For example, imagine a fictional premium tea brand called FineTeaz that targets young professionals in metropolitan settings who appreciate relaxing atmospheres and value mindfulness. The brand manager at FineTeaz might use the brand identity prism as follows to gain clarity on the various components of their brand identity and direct their brand efforts.

- **Physique:** Elegant, reusable packaging with earthy tones and minimalist design, reflecting calm and sustainability
- **Personality:** Warm, caring, and calm—a tone that encourages customers to slow down and enjoy the moment
- **Culture:** Focused on mindfulness and sustainable sourcing, showing a commitment to overall well-being
- **Self-image:** Customers see themselves as intentional and health-conscious, prioritizing self-care in their lives
- **Reflection:** Projects an image of serene, balanced individuals who value quality and mindfulness
- **Relationship:** Fosters a nurturing connection through personalized tea recommendations and thoughtful communication

By reflecting on each of the six brand identity prism components, the brand manager at FineTeaz will be able to communicate a cohesive identity. A cohesive brand identity via consistent visuals and messaging builds trust and sets the brand apart. It will also align with the values and aspirations of customers while simultaneously standing out in the saturated wellness market.

The Brand Identity Prism provides a structure for consistency and also acts as a valuable brand management tool that provides flexibility for adaptation. A brand manager should revisit the six components periodically to ensure that they align with shifting expectations and trends. For example, as sustainability becomes more important, brand managers may need to update messaging or packaging to reflect their environmental commitment.

3.2 Identifying Your Brand's Unique Value Proposition

A strong, unique value proposition (UVP) is crucial for a sustainable brand. It should clearly show why customers should pick your brand over others. It should also emphasize any unique benefits and values of your brand that resonate with the intended audience.

A brand's UVP should address the specific pain points, motivations, and aspirations of its audience directly. To refine it, brand managers must revisit the audience segments and customer personas they would have created earlier. Using these, they will be able to accurately define the attributes that their audience values most.

A strong UVP will be:

- **Specific:** Focused on concrete benefits rather than broad claims
- **Relevant:** Addresses the most important issues to your audience
- **Credible:** Supports your statements with evidence

For example, consider an Electric Vehicle (EV) manufacturer targeting urban professionals. Their UVP could state: *"Our EVs offer the longest range in their class and are made with 100% sustainable methods—perfect for eco-conscious urbanites."* This UVP addresses the audience's environmental and practical needs while showcasing the brand's focus on innovation and sustainability.

> **POINT TO REMEMBER**
>
> A strong UVP clearly communicates the unique benefits of a brand and is essential for differentiation in a competitive market.

3.2.1 Differentiation and credibility

In this section, we will discuss the concepts of brand differentiation and credibility and their relevance to the UVP.

To create an effective UVP, differentiation is essential. It refers to how your brand stands out in a crowded market. Brand managers must identify gaps in competitors' offerings and highlight what their brand does better or differently. This could include offering specialized features, enhanced service, or even a unique emotional appeal.

Credibility, on the other hand, means building trust in your brand by showing authenticity, expertise, or proven results. It helps customers believe in what you offer. It's important for brand managers to be able to support their UVPs with credible evidence such as:

- **Customer testimonials:** Real stories from satisfied customers add authenticity.
- **Case studies:** Highlight how your product or service solved a specific problem.
- **Certifications and awards:** External validation reinforces trust and credibility.

For example, a luxury mattress company could emphasize its UVP of superior comfort and support by sharing testimonials from athletes. These endorsements could show how the product improved their sleep and performance, giving customers a strong reason to trust the brand.

3.2.2 Tailoring the UVP for different segments

While the essence of your UVP should remain consistent, how it is expressed can and should be modified to resonate with different audience segments. Each segment may prioritize certain aspects of your offering over others, and tailoring your communication ensures relevance across diverse groups.

Imagine a high-performance sports drink brand with a UVP of "fueling endurance and recovery." For professional athletes, the emphasis could be on clinical-grade hydration and electrolyte formulas backed by research. For casual fitness enthusiasts, the messaging might focus on convenience, refreshing flavors, and all-day energy. The core UVP remains unchanged, but its delivery is tailored to meet the distinct priorities of each group.

DISCUSSION

Pick a brand that you are a fan of. Now, think of their top competitor. In what ways does the brand you picked offer a UVP that influences your decision to choose it over its top competitor?

3.2.3 The Value Proposition Canvas

The Value Proposition Canvas is a tool often used by brand managers to communicate their UVP effectively and align customer needs with what the brand offers. The value proposition canvas framework consists of two parts:

1. **Customer profile:** This part describes the tasks customers want to complete, the challenges they face, and the benefits they seek.

2. **Value map:** This explains how your products or services solve challenges and deliver benefits to customers.

Figure 3.2 Value proposition canvas

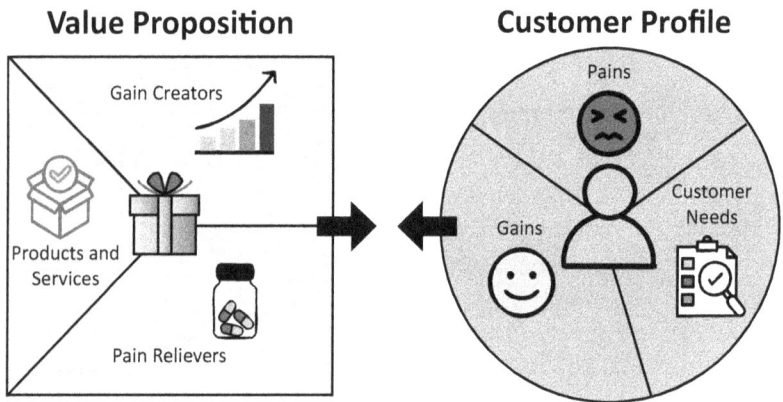

Source: Adapted from Osterwalder et al., 2014

By matching the elements of the customer profile with the value map, brand managers can ensure that their UVP addresses the most pressing concerns of their audience directly. This structured approach helps identify areas where a brand's offerings have the potential to create the most impact.

For example, consider a meal kit delivery company that targets busy working parents. Using the value proposition canvas, a brand manager might identify the following:

1. **Customer profile:** Parents want quick, healthy meals (customer needs), face challenges with time and dietary needs (pains), and desire convenience and nutritious options (gains).

2. **Value map:** The brand provides pre-portioned, ready-to-cook meal kits (pain relievers) and markets them as "family-tested recipes delivered to your door in under 30 minutes" (gain creators).

As a result, an effective UVP for this meal kit delivery company might be:

"Healthy meals made simple — nutritious, delicious, and family-approved, ready in just 30 minutes."

This UVP speaks directly to the needs of busy parents while differentiating the brand with its focus on family and convenience.

3.3 Visual Elements - Logos, Colors, and Typography

Visual elements act as the sensory foundation of a brand by creating impressions on customers before they even interact with a brand. These elements do more than make a brand recognizable; they also communicate personality, values, and promises at a glance. When applied consistently and effectively, the visual elements of a brand should create emotional connections. They should enhance recognition and reinforce trust.

3.3.1 Logos: The face of your brand

A logo is often the first thing customers see. It represents the brand's identity and purpose in a simple, visual way. A successful logo should be:

1. **Memorable:** Simple enough to be easily recalled
2. **Versatile:** Adaptable to different mediums, from business cards to social media icons
3. **Reflective:** Communicate a brand's mission and values

For example, a renewable energy startup might design a circular logo featuring clean lines and a sun motif. The circle can represent renewal, while the sun conveys energy and optimism. On the other hand, a logo that doesn't reflect the brand's values may confuse customers and damage its image. Regular feedback from customers helps ensure the logo connects with the target audience.

3.3.2 Colors: Emotional triggers

Colors play a crucial role in visual branding. They trigger emotions, shape perceptions, and affect buying decisions. Each color can have psychological associations.

While interpretation of color symbolism can vary, brand managers should be intentional in choosing colors that fit their brand's personality and appeal to their audience. For example, a wellness brand might use soothing earthy tones, while a technology brand might opt for bold blues and silvers to signal innovation. Figure 3.3 illustrates how certain colors may be associated with emotions.

Figure 3.3 Color association wheel

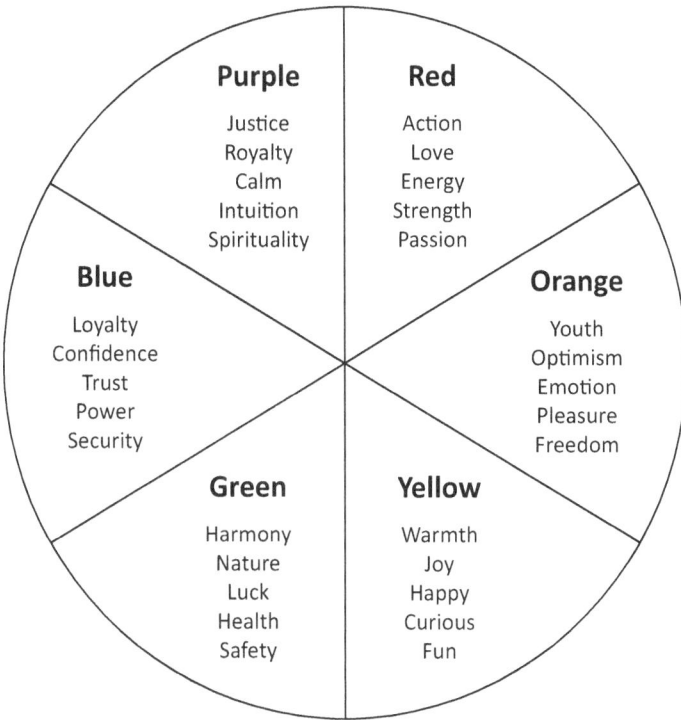

As shown in Figure 3.3 above, the color association wheel demonstrates some commonly associated traits and their respective colors. Managers can use this to ensure their brand image aligns with the message they wish to convey to customers.

To ensure that the colors reflect and convey the brand identity, brand managers can use the "C.L.E.A.R." framework when they are choosing colors.

- **Consistency:** Apply the same colors across platforms.
- **Logical alignment:** Choose colors that align with brand values.

- **Emotion:** Select colors that evoke the desired feelings.
- **Audience:** Reflect preferences and cultural connotations.
- **Recognition:** Ensure that colors are distinct within the industry.

3.3.3 Typography: Communication of personality

Typography conveys tone and personality through the choice of font. It influences how customers perceive a brand. Different fonts carry different connotations, for example:

- **Serif Fonts:** They are considered traditional and elegant (e.g., Times New Roman). Serif fonts are often used by corporate businesses such as law firms.
- **Sans-Serif Fonts:** They are known to be modern and approachable (e.g., Helvetica). Sans-serif fonts are popular with brands expressing innovation and newness, such as technology brands.
- **Display Fonts:** These are bold and distinctive fonts that should be used sparingly for impact, such as in logos and headlines.

An example of well-branded typography would be a children's educational website that uses round, playful fonts to convey friendliness and approachability. Conversely, a premium watch brand using that typography might come off as inexpensive and childish. To be aligned with its premium offering, the watch brand might use a sleek Serif font to express sophistication and luxury.

In practice, brand managers need to test typography for readability and appeal. They should also ensure that the typography conveys the same appearance across multiple touchpoints, such as desktop and mobile platforms.

Which element of a brand's identity (e.g., logo, color scheme, tone) do you typically find most memorable, and why?

3.3.4 Aligning all visual elements for brand harmony

Each visual element—logo, color, and typography—has its own role. Together, they impact how customers perceive the brand. Brand managers should make sure these elements work well together to create a clear, cohesive identity that connects with the audience.

Table 3.2 Visual elements in brand strategy

Visual Element	Purpose	Example
Logo	Identity and memorability	A circular logo symbolizing sustainability for an eco-brand
Color	Emotional connection	Blue for trust in financial services, green for sustainability
Typography	Tone and personality	Rounded Sans-serif for children's brands, Serif for luxury
Combined application	Cohesion across touchpoints	Fitness apparel using bold colors, dynamic logos, and modern fonts

Source: Adapted from Keller, 2013

Visual elements are more than just an aesthetic part of the brand. They are strategic tools for building brand identity and connecting with customers emotionally. They provide managers the opportunity to create a powerful and sustainable brand impression.

3.4 Brand Voice and Messaging

A brand voice is how the brand communicates, while messaging focuses on what it says. Together, they sculpt the brand's personality and communication style. These elements help the audience feel understood, valued, and connected. When used well, they create a consistent experience that builds trust and reinforces the brand's identity.

3.4.1 Brand voice

Brand voice refers to the distinct personality and style a brand uses across all interactions. It reflects the brand's identity and personality, developed in the early stages of brand building. It humanizes customer interactions by showing how the brand would communicate if it were a person. While the voice may adapt slightly across platforms (e.g., more casual on social media, more formal in reports), it should always be recognizable as part of the same brand.

A business or manager should consider the following questions when building their brand voice:

1. What is the tone of my brand? Is it formal, conversational, or playful?

2. What emotional response do I want it to invoke? Should it inspire, educate, entertain, or reassure?

3. Who is the primary audience? Consider the personas created in Chapter 2 and tailor the voice to resonate with their preferences.

A fitness app for millennials and Gen Z might use a lively, motivational voice: "Achieve your fitness goals with workouts designed for your busy life—your time and results matter." A financial advisory firm for professionals might take a calm, authoritative tone: "Secure your future with expert guidance tailored to your financial goals."

3.4.2 Brand messaging frameworks

A messaging framework is a set of key messages, tone, and style to ensure consistency and clarity in communication. It ensures consistency and focus in brand communication, regardless of platform or context. It ensures all messaging aligns with the brand's unique value proposition and goals.

Components of a messaging framework:

1. **Core message:** The overarching idea you want your audience to remember.
2. **Supporting messages:** Key benefits or proof points that reinforce the core message.
3. **Tone and style:** Adjustments for various platforms and audience segments to ensure relevancy and coherence.

3.4.3 Adapting messaging across channels

While the brand voice remains consistent across all platforms, the tone and style of delivery should adapt to the context and audience expectations for each channel.

Social media

The messaging on these platforms tends to be casual, engaging, and visually dynamic. Businesses can consider the use of humor, short videos, or interactive content to capture attention and drive interaction.

Website content

This channel requires a voice and messaging style that is typically more informative and action-oriented. Brand managers should focus on clarity, trustworthiness, and providing actionable information.

Customer support

The messaging style for customer support purposes should be reassuring and empathetic. This is an opportunity to address customer concerns with a helpful, understanding tone.

Adaptation doesn't mean changing the brand voice; it's about fine-tuning delivery for the audience and medium. This ensures that the core identity remains intact while increasing relevance and impact. Brand managers can use the "C.A.R.E." framework to tailor communication:

- **Consistency:** Maintain the brand voice across all channels.
- **Audience-centric:** Focus on what the specific audience values.
- **Relevance:** Adapt the tone and style to fit the context.
- **Engagement:** Encourage interaction and relationship-building.

3.5 Authenticity and Integrity

We live in a world where the internet provides prospective customers with essentially any information they seek, and skepticism among consumers is high. As a result, authenticity and integrity are extremely important for brand sustainability and consumer trust. Customers want to support brands that live their values and follow through on promises, remaining transparent even when challenges arise. Brands must assume that consumers will make it their mission to expose the truth behind brand claims. This makes it essential to remain true to the value and mission expressed by the brand.

Living your values

Brand managers must align their actions with the values stated by the brand. A fashion brand committed to ethical production, for example, could live its values by regularly highlighting partnerships with fair-trade suppliers and communicating narratives about the artisans behind the products.

Transparency and accountability

When brand managers encounter challenges, it's important to address them honestly. With information available practically everywhere, consumers will jump on any opportunity to expose a brand for conveying false truths, making it very challenging to sustain the brand in the long run.

The Trust Triangle Framework

Authenticity, consistency, and transparency form the foundation of trust. Brands that demonstrate all three attributes cultivate enduring customer loyalty:

1. **Authenticity:** Carrying out actions that align with brand promises.
2. **Consistency:** Delivering on promises repeatedly.
3. **Transparency:** Communicating openly about successes and setbacks.

Figure 3.4 The Trust Triangle

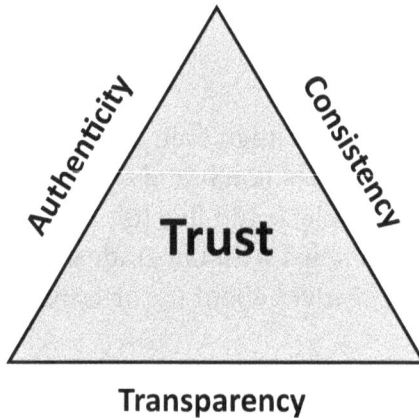

Source: Adapted from the general principles of brand trust and authenticity in Morgan and Hunt, 1994; Beverland, 2009; and Kotler and Keller, 2016).

Trust cannot be earned without building the walls of authenticity, consistency, and transparency. Authenticity isn't a one-time effort. It requires continuous alignment with customer values and expectations. Businesses and managers should regularly assess whether their practices, partnerships, and messaging reflect the principles that the intended audience cares about. Over time, this consistency fosters emotional loyalty, turning customers into advocates.

Building a sustainable brand goes beyond making a good first impression. It involves creating a cohesive identity based on understanding your customers and their values. This includes articulating a unique value proposition that meets their needs, designing visuals that reflect the brand's essence, using a genuine voice, and showing authenticity and integrity in every decision.

A sustainable brand evolves with its customers. It stays true to its core principles while adapting to trends and changing expectations. By applying these insights, you can build a brand that resonates today and stays relevant in the future.

As we conclude Chapter 3, you have a clear sense of how brand identity, audience insights, and a strong UVP can power a brand. You've learned the foundational concepts like brand identity, awareness, and reputation. You also gained a clear understanding of your audience and built a cohesive brand identity with a strong UVP. These steps lay the groundwork for sustainable success.

Next, with this foundational knowledge under your belt, you'll turn these insights into practical action. In Chapter 4, we'll explore brand audits, positioning, and flexible planning to keep your brand competitive while staying true to its core values.

Chapter Summary

- A sustainable brand connects with its audience, stands out in the market, and adapts to changes over time.

- Brand identity is how the brand is seen externally and the values it reflects internally.

- Kapferer's Brand Identity Prism defines six key elements: physique, personality, culture, self-image, reflection, and relationship. A cohesive brand identity requires consistency across all six elements.

- Outward-facing elements like physique and reflection are part of externalization. Internal-facing elements like personality and culture fall under internalization.

- A unique value proposition (UVP) explains why customers should choose your brand and whether it addresses their specific needs.

- Strong UVPs are clear, relevant, and backed by evidence like reviews or certifications.

- The Value Proposition Canvas matches customer needs with brand solutions to ensure relevance.

- Logos, colors, and typography create emotional connections and make a brand recognizable.

- Colors should align with the brand's personality and trigger emotions that fit the audience.

- Typography sets the tone and affects how professional, approachable, or creative the brand appears.

- A brand's voice defines its communication style, while messaging ensures consistency across all channels.

- Adapting messaging for different platforms helps maintain relevance while staying true to the brand.

- Authenticity and integrity are essential for trust and require actions to match stated values.

- The Trust Triangle—authenticity, consistency, and transparency—builds loyalty and long-term trust.

Quiz

1. **What is the primary purpose of Kapferer's Brand Identity Prism?**

    a. To create product packaging designs

    b. To define a cohesive and multidimensional brand identity

    c. To track brand performance metrics

    d. To identify customer pain points

2. **Which of the following is NOT a component of the Brand Identity Prism?**

    a. Personality

    b. Culture

    c. Vision

    d. Reflection

3. **What does the "internalization" axis in the Brand Identity Prism focus on?**

    a. Outward projection of the brand

    b. How the brand aligns with an audience's self-concept and values

    c. Competitor analysis

    d. Physical attributes of the brand

4. **In the Brand Identity Prism, which component reflects how customers see themselves when interacting with the brand?**

    a. Reflection

    b. Physique

    c. Relationship

    d. Self-image

5. Which of these is an example of "Physique" in the Brand Identity Prism?
   a. Friendly tone of voice
   b. Sleek logo design and minimalist packaging
   c. Commitment to sustainable sourcing
   d. Image of customers as adventurous

6. A brand with a nurturing personality most likely wants to:
   a. Evoke excitement and adventure
   b. Reflect care and emotional support
   c. Emphasize boldness and innovation
   d. Promote exclusivity and luxury

7. What does the "Culture" component of the Brand Identity Prism represent?
   a. The values and principles underpinning the brand
   b. The visual design elements of the brand
   c. The behavior of the brand's customers
   d. The tone of communication with customers

8. How does the Brand Identity Prism help brand managers?
   a. By analyzing competitors' marketing strategies
   b. By aligning external messaging with internal values
   c. By identifying key financial metrics
   d. By creating sales plans

9. A compelling Unique Value Proposition (UVP) should be:
   a. General and broad
   b. Specific, relevant, and credible
   c. Focused on product features only
   d. Centered on price reduction

10. Which tool aligns customer pains, gains, and jobs to be done with a brand's solutions?
    a. SWOT Analysis
    b. Value Proposition Canvas
    c. Trust Triangle Framework
    d. Brand Identity Prism

Answers

1 – b	2 – a	3 – b	4 – d	5 – b
6 – b	7 – a	8 – b	9 – b	10 – b

CHAPTER 4

Brand Strategy and Positioning

Key Learning Objectives

- Learn to align brand goals with actionable strategies and prioritize resources for sustained growth.
- Understand how to evaluate brand performance through audits and refine strategies based on findings.
- Explore techniques for building a unique value proposition and differentiating from competitors.
- Discover methods to maintain relevance in a dynamic market and adapt strategies without losing brand identity.

A brand's success depends on more than understanding its audience and creating a sustainable identity. It also requires strategic market positioning and well-planned execution for long-term growth. This chapter covers tools and techniques that help brand managers create practical, sustainable strategies. A strategic brand plan acts as a flexible guide to achieve goals while adapting to market changes.

You will discover how regular brand audits ensure that efforts match goals and customer needs. You will also learn how strong positioning helps a brand stand out and stay relevant in a competitive market. By the end of this chapter, you will know how to create a strategic plan and measure brand performance.

4.1 Building a Strategic Brand Plan

A strategic brand plan guides managers in aligning brand efforts with business objectives effectively. It combines customer insights, competitor analysis, and clear goals. These elements help a brand manager create a plan that makes the brand indispensable to its audience while staying flexible in a changing market. This ensures both consistency and long-term relevance.

4.1.1 Elements of a strategic brand plan

Combining the knowledge and tools presented in previous chapters, we can now create an effective and strategic brand plan. Every plan will be unique to the brand. However, all successful brand plans share the following fundamental components. The core elements to consider in a brand plan include:

1. **Vision and mission statements**

   These statements articulate your brand's purpose and direction:

   - **Vision:** The long-term goal your brand strives to achieve.
   - **Mission:** A clear statement of your brand's purpose and the actions it will take to achieve its vision.

2. **Brand objectives**

   These objectives should be SMART—specific, measurable, achievable, relevant, and time-bound. Examples include increasing awareness, boosting customer retention, or growing market share.

3. **Customer insights and target segments**

   Insights gathered in Chapter 2 about customer segments, aspirations, and pain points should inform every decision in the brand plan. Tailor strategies for each segment to ensure meaningful engagement.

4. **Unique value proposition (UVP)**

   The UVP developed in Chapter 3 should take center stage, guiding all messaging and product development decisions. A strategic brand plan ensures this UVP is communicated consistently across all channels.

5. **Competitive analysis**

   Understanding competitors is key to positioning your brand effectively. Identify areas where they fall short and look for opportunities to stand out.

4.1.2 The process of strategic brand planning

Strategic brand planning follows the clear steps outlined below to turn goals into actionable strategies:

Step 1: Define long-term goals

You can begin by setting clear objectives for the next 3–5 years. Use SMART goals from Chapter 1 to focus on objectives like becoming a market leader or shaping brand perception.

Step 2: Develop short-term milestones

Next, break long-term goals into smaller, actionable steps. These milestones help track progress and keep teams focused.

Step 3: Map strategic initiatives

Plan specific projects to achieve your goals. Examples include launching a product, enhancing customer support, or entering a new market.

Step 4: Allocate resources

Assign time, budget, and personnel to execute each initiative effectively.

Step 5: Measure and adapt

Regularly review performance metrics to evaluate progress. Adjust strategies based on data to keep the plan flexible and aligned with evolving needs.

4.1.3 Cross-functional alignment

A strategic brand plan needs alignment across all departments. Marketing, sales, customer service, and product development must collaborate to ensure a consistent brand experience.

For example, a skincare brand launching a new product line should also focus on:

- **Marketing:** Highlights the eco-friendly ingredients in campaigns
- **Sales:** Communicates the UVP effectively during in-store promotions

- **Customer service:** Educates customers about product benefits and usage
- **Product development:** Ensures the packaging reflects sustainable practices

Brand managers should maintain a strong rapport with co-existing departments and conduct regular cross-functional meetings. This ensures that everyone understands their role in achieving the established strategic objectives.

4.1.4 Make the brand plan flexible

Markets are always changing, and brands must adapt to meet evolving customer needs and trends. A flexible brand plan helps address challenges and seize new opportunities. This can be accomplished using methods such as scenario planning and iterative updates.

Scenario planning

Businesses should plan ahead for potential challenges. They should develop strategies to address disruptions such as supply chain problems or shifts in customer behavior. Preparation helps brands respond effectively to unexpected crises.

For example, a travel brand might adapt to global events like COVID-19 by shifting its focus from international trips to domestic staycation packages. A strong plan ensures the brand can respond quickly to such changes.

Iterative updates

This involves scheduling regular strategy reviews to assess progress and make adjustments. Without measuring progress, brand managers cannot know what changes should be implemented to optimize the strategy and keep a brand sustainable.

DISCUSSION What are some strategies you believe could be effective in keeping a brand relevant amid changing market trends?

4.2 Conducting a Brand Audit

A brand audit reviews how a brand performs in the market. It identifies strengths, weaknesses, and opportunities.

Regular audits help brand managers see how customers view the brand. They help to check if promises are being met and compare the brand to competitors. These insights guide improvements and keep the brand aligned with customer needs.

4.2.1 The purpose of a brand audit

A brand audit keeps the brand relevant, competitive, and consistent. Brand managers should ask key questions, such as:

1. Does the brand's identity align with its values and promises?
2. Are customers engaging with the brand as expected?
3. How does the brand compare to competitors?
4. Check for gaps between customer expectations and their actual experience.

Identifying strengths and weaknesses helps businesses focus on areas with the most potential for improvement.

4.2.2 Components of a brand audit

A brand audit involves internal and external reviews, competitor analysis, customer feedback, and performance metrics (Kotler & Keller, 2016). Each component is explored below in detail:

Internal assessment

An internal assessment is a detailed review of a brand's mission, vision, values, and identity. It confirms that these elements align with strategic objectives and remain consistent across all brand activities.

External perception

An external perception analysis looks at how the customers and the market view the brand. This includes evaluation of reviews, feedback on social media, and third-party assessments to see where the brand stands in public opinion.

Competitive analysis

A competitive analysis compares a brand's pricing, messaging, customer experience, and product features to those of competing brands. Identifying what sets the brand apart allows managers to highlight unique strengths and address weaknesses, if any.

Customer feedback

Collecting customer feedback through surveys, focus groups, and interviews reveals satisfaction levels, unmet needs, and perceptions of brand strengths or weaknesses. These insights guide adjustments to products or services.

Performance metrics

Performance metrics, such as market share, retention rates, and website traffic, offer quantifiable measures of success. Regular tracking of these metrics helps managers evaluate progress and refine strategies.

Table 4.1 Brand audit checklist

Component	Key questions to address
Internal assessment	Are the brand's mission and identity consistent?
External perception	How do customers perceive the brand?
Competitive analysis	What differentiates us from competitors?
Customer feedback	Are there unmet customer needs or expectations?
Performance metrics	Are we meeting our strategic objectives?

4.2.3 Brand audit tools

Brand managers use several tools to gather insights and assess performance. Below are five key methods commonly used in a brand audit to guide strategic decisions.

SWOT Analysis

A SWOT analysis utilizes a brand's Strengths, Weaknesses, Opportunities, and Threats to assess internal and external performance-related factors.

Figure 4.1 SWOT analysis

S

STRENGTHS
Internal attributes and resources that support a successful outcome.

W

WEAKNESSES
Internal factors that might hinder an organization's ability to achieve its objectives.

O

OPPORTUNITIES
External factors that the organization can capitalize on or use to its advantages.

T

THREATS
External factors that could cause trouble for the business or project.

Source: Adapted from Porter, 1980.

Customer surveys

Brand managers can collect quantitative and qualitative data from customer surveys to get a sense of customer satisfaction and brand performance.

Sentiment analysis tools

Organizations should make it a frequent practice to analyze social media and online reviews. Doing so will allow them to gauge public sentiment about their brand.

Website analytics

A brand's website gives key data for audits. Metrics like bounce rate, page views, and conversion rates demonstrate how well digital touchpoints perform.

Benchmarking

Benchmarking means comparing your brand's metrics to industry standards or top competitors. This helps brand managers see how the brand is doing in the market.

> **DISCUSSION**
>
> Think of a small, local business brand you are familiar with. How would you go about performing a brand audit for them, and what key areas would you focus on? Why?

4.3 Positioning and Competition

Positioning creates a special place for your brand in customers' minds. It highlights what sets your brand apart and aligns with customers' needs and values. This section explains how to define and refine your brand's position while managing competition.

4.3.1 Brand positioning

Brand positioning is how customers perceive your brand compared to others. A well-positioned brand gains stronger recognition and deeper loyalty. It also stands a better chance of converting new customers.

When positioning a brand, follow these five steps:

Step 1: Identify key attributes

Find out which attributes matter most to your target audience, like quality, price, or sustainability. Brand managers can prioritize these by reviewing customer research and feedback.

Step 2: Conduct a competitive analysis

After identifying key attributes, proceed to map competitors' positioning. Identify their strengths and look for opportunities to stand out.

Step 3: Define your positioning statement

A positioning statement clearly explains what makes the brand different. To be effective, it should include:

1. **Target audience:** The specific segment your brand serves
2. **Frame of reference:** The category in which your brand competes
3. **Point of differentiation:** What sets your brand apart
4. **Key benefit:** The primary value your brand delivers

Example of a positioning statement:

"For environmentally conscious consumers (target audience) looking for premium coffee (frame of reference), we offer single-origin, carbon-neutral beans (point of differentiation) that let you enjoy a rich cup of coffee while protecting the planet (key benefit)."

Step 4: Validate your position

With the positioning statement finalized, brand managers should begin testing their position. This could be accomplished via focus groups or customer surveys, which provide insight to measure alignment with audience preferences.

Step 5: Communicate your position

Finally, the brand manager should ensure that finalized brand positioning is communicated effectively at every touchpoint.

POINT TO REMEMBER Effective positioning distinguishes a brand by highlighting its unique attributes and competitive advantages.

Table 4.2 Positioning statement framework

Element	Description	Example
Target audience	Whom does your brand serve	Environmentally conscious consumers
Frame of reference	The category your brand belongs to	Premium coffee
Point of differentiation	What makes your brand unique	Single-origin, carbon-neutral beans
Key benefit	The main value your brand delivers	Enjoy a rich cup of coffee while protecting the planet

Source: Adapted from Porter, 1996.

FUN FACT

Domino's Pizza once ran a campaign admitting its shortcomings. This unexpected move helped rebuild customer trust and reposition the brand as a trustworthy and relatable competitor.

4.3.2 Perceptual mapping

A perceptual map is a visual positioning tool that shows how customers view your brand compared to competitors based on key attributes.

To create a perceptual map:

1. Identify two attributes that are highly relevant to your industry (e.g., price and quality).

2. Plot competitors on a two-dimensional grid based on how they rank in these attributes.

3. Assess where your brand fits and look for gaps on the map; these aid in identifying opportunities where competition is minimal.

Figure 4.2 Perceptual map

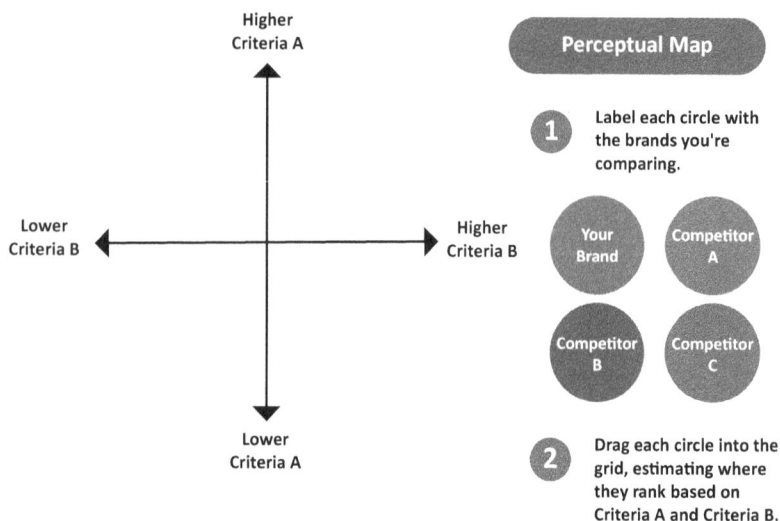

Source: Adapted from Kotler & Keller, 2016.

4.3.3 Competing through differentiation

Differentiation is the key to effective positioning. Offering something unique that customers value gives them a strong reason to choose your brand. Differentiation can come from product features, customer experience, or emotional connection:

Product features

To differentiate via product features, a business might opt to highlight innovative features such as patented technology to set them apart from their competitors.

Customer experience

A brand can also be differentiated from competitors by offering better service, faster delivery, or optimized user experience.

Emotional connection

Brands can stand out by building relationships with their audience through shared values like sustainability or inclusivity.

Competitors often try to imitate or surpass a successful brand. Brand managers must innovate, encourage customer loyalty, and watch the competition. This helps them respond proactively instead of reacting too late.

4.4 Maintaining Relevance

The market constantly changes under the influence of customer demands, new competitors, technology, and cultural shifts. Relevance means the alignment between a brand and its customers' evolving preferences and values. Brands that rely on past success risk losing relevance.

A relevant brand is one that meets the following three criteria:

1. Solves current problems or addresses unmet needs
2. Reflects the cultural and societal values of its audience
3. Innovates to stay ahead of trends and competitors

4.4.1 Adapting to changing customer expectations

Customer needs change with lifestyles, economic shifts, and new technology. To stay relevant, brand managers should:

- **Monitor trends:** Use research, social listening, and industry reports to track changes in customer behavior.
- **Act on feedback:** Collect and analyze customer input to find areas for improvement.

- **Experiment and innovate:** Test new ideas, products, or services that align with emerging needs.

Relevance doesn't require abandoning a brand's identity. Instead, it means adjusting offerings and messaging while staying true to core values. By building on what customers already trust and value, brand managers can meet evolving preferences effectively.

4.4.2 Tools for staying relevant

There are several tools and strategies available for brand managers that can assist in maintaining relevance. Below are some common methods managers use and rely on to monitor relevance:

Trend mapping

This involves visualizing how customer preferences and market trends have evolved with time. Using trend mapping, businesses can identify where the capabilities of their brand and emerging demands or trends meet.

Scenario planning

Brand managers can anticipate potential market changes by developing scenarios based on external factors like economic shifts, technology breakthroughs, or cultural movements. They should ensure they develop flexible strategies to respond to each scenario.

Competitor benchmarking

Regularly reviewing competitors' activities helps businesses spot threats and opportunities, keeping the brand distinct and competitive.

4.4.3 Measuring relevance

Relevance is tracked using KPIs that show how well your brand connects with its audience.

1. **Engagement metrics:** They monitor interaction rates on social media, emails, and other channels.
2. **Market share:** It reflects your brand's standing relative to competitors.
3. **Product or service usage:** Measures adoption rates for new offerings or updates.
4. **Sentiment analysis:** Analyzes customer attitudes expressed in reviews, surveys, or social media mentions.

Table 4.3 Relevance metrics and their applications

Metric	What it measures	Application
Engagement metrics	Customer interaction and interest	Evaluate campaign effectiveness and refine communication
Market share	Competitive standing	Understand overall positioning and opportunities for growth
Product usage	Adoption of new features	Measure the success of innovations and identify needed adjustments
Sentiment analysis	Customer attitudes	Address concerns and leverage positive feedback

Source: Adapted from Aaker, 2014.

Relevance is an ongoing effort. It involves knowing your audience, adapting to market shifts, and embracing new ideas. Successful businesses balance innovation with authenticity, keeping their brand meaningful in a fast-changing market.

Chapter Summary

- A strategic brand plan acts as a roadmap for reaching goals, guided by vision and mission.
- Effective planning involves setting objectives, studying competitors, and watching market trends.
- Strategic planning and flexibility support long-term brand success in dynamic markets.
- A brand audit uncovers strengths, weaknesses, opportunities, and threats to gauge current and future performance.
- Internal audits: Check team alignment, culture, and how well brand values are followed.
- External audits: Look at how customers see the brand, how it's positioned in the market, and how it compares to rivals.
- Positioning highlights what sets your brand apart, focusing on unique value.
- Competitive analysis identifies rivals and reviews their strengths, weaknesses, and strategies.
- Differentiation delivers unique benefits or emotional connections that others don't offer.
- Tools like SWOT analysis and perceptual mapping measure performance and inform strong strategies.
- Staying relevant involves adapting to customer needs, market trends, and evolving technology.
- Monitoring trends and gathering feedback help brands plan for change and remain competitive.
- Consistent follow-through on promises builds trust and loyalty, even in shifting markets.
- Balancing authenticity with innovation keeps the brand aligned with its core values while meeting new demands.

Quiz

1. **What is the primary purpose of a strategic brand plan?**
   a. To develop a product roadmap
   b. To align brand efforts with business objectives and ensure long-term relevance
   c. To outline marketing strategies only
   d. To reduce competition

2. **What does the UVP in a strategic brand plan stand for?**
   a. Unique Value Proposition
   b. Unified Vision Plan
   c. Universal Value Principle
   d. Unique Vision Priority

3. **Which of the following is NOT a key component of a strategic brand plan?**
   a. Mission statement
   b. Customer insights
   c. Perceptual mapping
   d. Competitive analysis

4. **What is the first step in strategic brand planning?**
   a. Conducting a brand audit
   b. Defining long-term goals
   c. Allocating resources
   d. Mapping strategic initiatives

5. Why is cross-functional alignment important for a strategic brand plan?
   a. It reduces employee workload
   b. It ensures all departments work cohesively toward brand objectives
   c. It eliminates the need for customer feedback
   d. It focuses solely on marketing teams

6. What is the purpose of scenario planning in brand strategy?
   a. To identify customer pain points
   b. To develop contingency plans for potential disruptions
   c. To assess internal brand identity
   d. To improve employee communication

7. What is the purpose of a brand audit?
   a. To establish a new target audience
   b. To evaluate the brand's position and identify areas of improvement
   c. To create a new value proposition
   d. To enhance product design

8. Which of the following is NOT part of a brand audit?
   a. Customer feedback
   b. Internal assessment
   c. Social media advertising
   d. Performance metrics

9. What is the role of a SWOT analysis in a brand audit?
   a. To analyze the design of a logo
   b. To assess strengths, weaknesses, opportunities, and threats
   c. To map competitor pricing strategies
   d. To measure social media engagement

10. A perceptual map is a tool used to:
   a. Visualize brand values
   b. Understand customer personas
   c. Plot competitors based on attributes like price and quality
   d. Track market share over time

Answers

1 – b	2 – a	3 – c	4 – b	5 – b
6 – b	7 – b	8 – c	9 – b	10 – c

CHAPTER 5

The Science Behind Effective Branding

Key Learning Objectives

- Identify how cognitive and emotional processes influence brand perception at both conscious and subconscious levels.
- Explain how emotional drivers, selective attention, and priming create deeper brand connections.
- Explore the role of trust and loyalty in long-term brand success.
- Examine neuroscientific principles, including reward pathways, habit loops, and biases.
- Apply ethical frameworks for influencing decisions through choice architecture, honest persuasion, and authentic storytelling.

Branding is often celebrated for its artistic flair. Ever pause to wonder why certain logos or taglines stick in your mind for years? The reason goes deeper than pretty designs; it touches on how our brains interpret and store brand messages. Genuine effectiveness in brand management relies on more than artistic elements alone.

Research in consumer psychology and neuroscience indicates that people notice, interpret, and recall brand messages via complex mental processes that operate both consciously and below awareness (Kotler & Keller, 2016; Plassmann et al., 2012).

As we've explored in previous chapters, a brand's success depends not just on its external appeal but also on how well it aligns with consumer perceptions and emotional connections. Building on these foundations, in this chapter, you will explore the science behind branding, examining how cognitive processes, emotional triggers, and subconscious influences shape consumer behavior and brand decision-making.

Beginning with an overview of the role of emotions in brand attachments, you will explore how loyalty and trust arise (and can be sustained over time). We will then move to the neuroscience at play, where you will learn how reward systems, subconscious cues, and cognitive biases shape preferences. Finally, readers will dive into the art of ethically influencing decisions as brand managers, blending choice architecture, transparent persuasion, and genuine storytelling.

5.1 The Role of Emotions in Brand Management

Consumer brand decisions may appear rational and based on cost comparisons or product features, but countless studies suggest that feelings often overshadow straightforward logic when people select which brands to embrace (Fournier, 1998).

A product can boast the highest technical quality in its category, yet if it fails to provide a sense of warmth, excitement, or trust, its advantages may risk going unnoticed.

Emotions help consumers form connections beyond transactions. Emotions are what differentiate a one-time purchase from a lasting relationship.

In this section, we will explore the emotional forces behind brand engagement. You will learn how subconscious processes such as "selective attention" and "priming" can fuel those connections and how brand managers and businesses can use these influences to set themselves apart in a crowded market.

5.1.1 Emotional drivers

Emotions shape how consumers perceive and engage with brands. The impact of consumer emotions influences everything from their initial interest to long-term loyalty. Logical factors like price and quality matter. However, emotional connections are what often drive purchasing decisions and brand advocacy. Brand managers can create more meaningful relationships with their audience by tapping into these specific emotional drivers:

1. **Nostalgia:** Positive memories of the past that can be used to create emotional connections
2. **Belonging:** A sense of community and shared identity among consumers
3. **Empathy and care:** Demonstrating genuine understanding and concern for customer needs

Let's discuss these emotional drivers further in-depth:

1. Nostalgia

Nostalgia can transport people back to a simpler or happier time. Brands often tap into this by reviving retro packaging or referencing past pop-culture moments

(Holbrook & Schindler, 2003). Think of a cereal brand bringing back its original box design from decades ago. This sparks warm memories of childhood mornings.

2. Belonging

Humans crave social bonds. Communities can form around brands that cultivate a sense of shared identity or purpose. It could be a coffee chain that fosters a warm café culture or an apparel line that throws local meetups. These gatherings encourage customers to feel part of something bigger than themselves.

TIP Let nostalgia emerge naturally. When it aligns with authentic brand values, it can create powerful connections without coming off as a cheap marketing ploy.

Example: Starbucks nurtures belonging by inviting customers to customize their drinks and share the results online. This personal involvement fosters a community of coffee fans who identify with the brand's overall vibe.

3. Empathy and Care

Many brands earn loyalty by genuinely showing they understand their audience's struggles or passions. From healthcare apps sharing real users' success stories to clothing lines launching adaptive designs, empathy helps customers feel seen and supported (Aaker, 1997). It's less about pushing products and more about offering comfort and understanding.

| Table 5.1 | Emotional drivers |

Emotional driver	Definition	Example
Nostalgia	Tying products to beloved past experiences	Throwback packaging or limited edition 'retro' ads
Belonging	Building community and shared identity	Meetups, hashtags, and lifestyle affiliations
Empathy	Showing genuine care for customers' challenges	Inclusive sizing, accessible product design

DISCUSSION

Think of a brand that you feel emotionally connected to. Which of the emotional drivers (nostalgia, belonging, or empathy) do you think contributes most to your connection with that brand? Why?

5.1.2 Selective attention and priming as emotional entry points

With so many messages flooding our senses daily, it's impossible to process them all. That's where "selective attention" comes in (Kahneman, 1973). We naturally filter out anything that doesn't match our current goals or interests. A running-shoe ad is more likely to stand out if you're already browsing for exercise tips.

"Priming" is the subtle way prior cues shape our next perception (Bargh & Chartrand, 2000). Imagine a luxury hotel website that uses calming images and soft music. Even before you enter the actual hotel, your mind has been primed to associate this brand with relaxation.

> **POINT TO REMEMBER** Selective attention helps a brand message get noticed, while priming influences how it's interpreted. Together, they set the emotional stage before consumers even start rationally comparing features or prices.

Combining selective attention and priming highlights how emotions can take hold well before a consumer has weighed the pros and cons of a purchase. Recognizing that people process brand messages through filters influenced by current interests and subtle prompts allows brand managers to create impactful experiences.

5.1.3 Emotional differentiation

When multiple brands have similar offerings, emotions become the deciding factor in the consumer's choice. While logic can justify a purchase, emotional connection strengthens brand loyalty.

In Chapter 3, we learned how visual elements like color and imagery help shape emotional connections by triggering subconscious associations. Recall that a strong visual identity promotes recognition and emotional appeal. This impact is maximized when paired with compelling storytelling.

1. **Storytelling as a differentiator**

   Storytelling allows a brand to craft personal narratives that resonate with consumers. A well-created story transforms a product into something relatable and memorable. This reinforces brand values in an authentic way.

Example: Instead of listing a camera's technical features, a camera brand might follow the journey of a world-traveling photographer. This would showcase the camera as a tool for adventure and self-expression. Emotional framing like this makes the product more than just a device. Instead, it is a gateway to experiences.

By combining strong visual branding with engaging narratives, brands create emotional bonds that extend beyond transactions. This makes consumers more likely to stay loyal even when competitors offer similar products.

2. **Consistent emotional value**

A brand's emotional appeal should not be situational or inconsistent. Businesses should reinforce their core message across all customer touchpoints. Some brands center their identity around playfulness, urging customers to bring fun into their routines. Others focus on calm and restoration, shaping environments that reduce stress.

Example: The toy production company, "Lego," constantly reinforces creativity and imagination in all its messaging, from advertisements to in-store experiences.

Mixed signals can damage emotional differentiation. A spa brand promoting relaxation but sending daily promotional emails can disrupt the intended experience. This makes consumers feel bombarded rather than relaxed.

3. Practice what you preach

A brand's emotional appeal should align with its real-world actions. If a company claims to prioritize sustainability but continues using excessive plastic packaging, its messaging falls flat. This will lead to consumer distrust.

Example: Patagonia strengthens its emotional connection by actively advocating for environmental causes. Unlike brands that simply talk about sustainability, Patagonia backs up its message by using recycled materials. It donates a percentage of its profits to conservation efforts. This consistency helps in strengthening brand loyalty as customers see a real alignment between the company's words and actions.

TIP Ensure that brand actions align with emotional messaging. Consumers will notice when a brand's values and behavior don't match.

Conversely, brands that fail to follow through on their values may risk alienating customers. A company that claims, "We care about families," but doesn't offer family-friendly policies or services, weakens its emotional credibility.

5.2 Earning Loyalty and Trust

A brand might catch someone's eye once, but winning long-term loyalty requires trust (Morgan & Hunt, 1994). Trust emerges gradually through reliable performance, honest communication, and consistent follow-through on promises. When consumers see the same positive experience repeated or see the brand "own up" to mistakes in a straightforward way, they tend to give it the benefit of the doubt.

5.2.1 Building trust through brand actions

Brand consistency goes beyond a matching color scheme or logo. It's about delivering the same level of quality or support each time people interact with you. If you claim that your sportswear line uses ultra-durable fabric, customers expect that promise to hold. Failing to meet these expectations sparks "cognitive dissonance," the mental discomfort we feel when our beliefs clash with reality (Festinger, 1957).

Example: Pepsi's 2017 ad featuring Kendall Jenner tried to align itself with social activism but came off as tone-deaf. Many viewers felt the commercial trivialized important social issues. This created a visible mismatch between Pepsi's stated message and its actual actions.

On the flip side, a brand that repeatedly matches its words with results solidifies trust. Nike, for instance, has consistently championed athlete empowerment and stood behind bold campaigns, even those sparking controversy. This reinforces their brand image in a way that resonates with core consumers.

Trust through transparency

Modern consumers do their homework. They read reviews, examine ingredient lists, and check whether companies honor ethical or environmental commitments. Being open about sourcing, labor practices, and costs sends out a clear signal of honesty. Apple, for instance, publishes transparency reports on data privacy to show it takes such concerns seriously (Kotler & Keller, 2016). While transparency cannot promise perfection, it does show customers a willingness to keep them informed.

Brand trust is built over time but can be lost instantly. Businesses should always prioritize consistency between messaging and real-world brand experiences to maintain credibility. Acknowledging mistakes or lapses can also promote trust. For example, a food and beverage company facing quality issues might release an immediate statement explaining the nature of the problem and how it plans to fix it. A proactive response often impresses consumers more than silence or denial.

Figure 5.1 demonstrates how a combination of consistent and transparent brand actions generates the highest level of consumer trust.

Figure 5.1 Trust building matrix

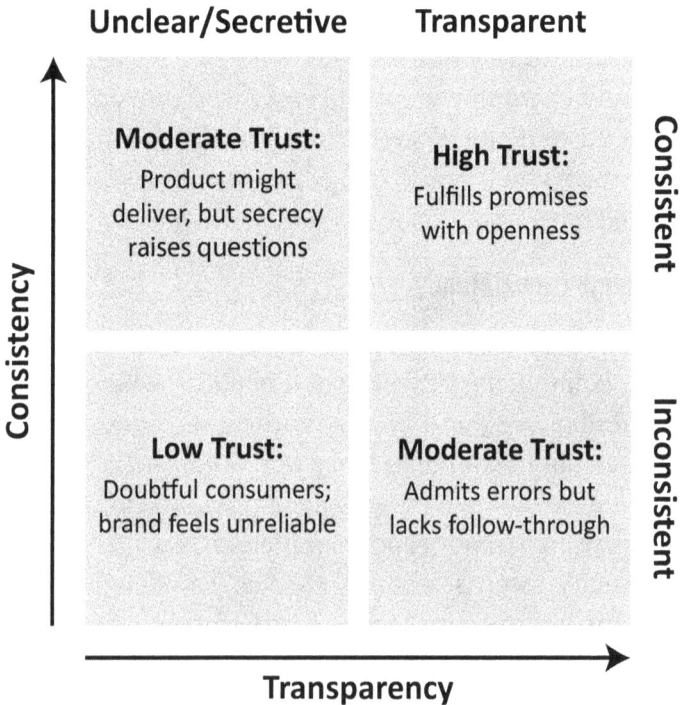

	Unclear/Secretive	Transparent	
Consistency ↑	**Moderate Trust:** Product might deliver, but secrecy raises questions	**High Trust:** Fulfills promises with openness	Consistent
	Low Trust: Doubtful consumers; brand feels unreliable	**Moderate Trust:** Admits errors but lacks follow-through	Inconsistent

Transparency →

5.2.2 Why trust leads to loyalty

When people trust a brand, minor hiccups, for instance, a delayed shipment or a missed feature, won't automatically prompt them to jump ship. The overall feeling of reliability, fairness, and transparency often outweighs isolated annoyances. Think of Amazon Prime members who stay loyal despite occasional late deliveries; they trust that, most of the time, Amazon delivers convenience and value.

Word of mouth magic

Trustworthy brands also benefit from organic recommendations. People love telling friends about a positive experience. It feels good to share something genuinely helpful or exciting. These personal endorsements often carry more weight than any advertisement ever could (Kotler & Keller, 2016).

Building communities through online groups, local events, or user-generated content deepens that sense of shared identity. Customers talk amongst themselves, helping each other out, sharing brand experiences, and strengthening that emotional bond. Loyalty then becomes more about belonging to a network than just using a product.

5.2.3 Recovering from setbacks

Even brands with the best intentions encounter occasional crises, from product recalls to Public Relations (PR) missteps. How a company responds in the first few hours or days can shape consumer perceptions for years.

Handling public backlash with transparency

When a crisis arises, some brands attempt to minimize or conceal the issue, hoping it will fade. However, today's consumers expect immediate accountability. Brands that acknowledge mistakes early and publicly tend to recover more effectively.

Rebuilding credibility

Apologies alone don't restore trust. Brands must pair words with action by taking meaningful corrective steps such as:

- Offering refunds or replacements
- Implementing new safety measures
- Providing regular updates on how the company is improving

Example: Chipotle Mexican Grill faced repeated food safety issues in 2015 but rebuilt consumer confidence by overhauling its supply chain, implementing stricter food handling policies, and offering free food promotions to win back customers.

> **POINT TO REMEMBER** A well-handled crisis can strengthen brand loyalty if customers see real effort toward improvement.

5.3 Neuroscience in Branding: Understanding Consumer Behavior

Even though people often talk about "rational" buying motives like price or product specifications, research in neuroscience shows that subconscious processes drive much of our decision-making (Plassmann et al., 2012). When brand managers understand these hidden drivers, it's easier to craft brand experiences that feel intuitive and enjoyable rather than pushy.

5.3.1 Reward pathways and habit formation

Any time we have a rewarding experience, our brains release dopamine, a neurotransmitter that signals, "Hey, let's do that again!" (Schmitt, 1999). Brands can tap into this by designing small moments of delight. A delightful unboxing experience, for instance, or a loyalty perk that surprises you at checkout, can trigger those "feel-good" brain chemicals.

"Habit loops" take this further (Duhigg, 2012). They're built on a "cue" (like a recognizable logo), a "routine" (browsing the brand's website), and a "reward" (feeling stylish, productive, or otherwise satisfied). If a brand consistently delivers that reward, consumers begin returning to it almost automatically.

A cue, such as one's morning alarm, triggers a routine, enjoying a morning coffee in this case. The result of the routine is a feeling of productivity, which releases feel-good brain chemicals and triggers the person to repeat the action in the future.

Figure 5.2 Habit-loop diagram

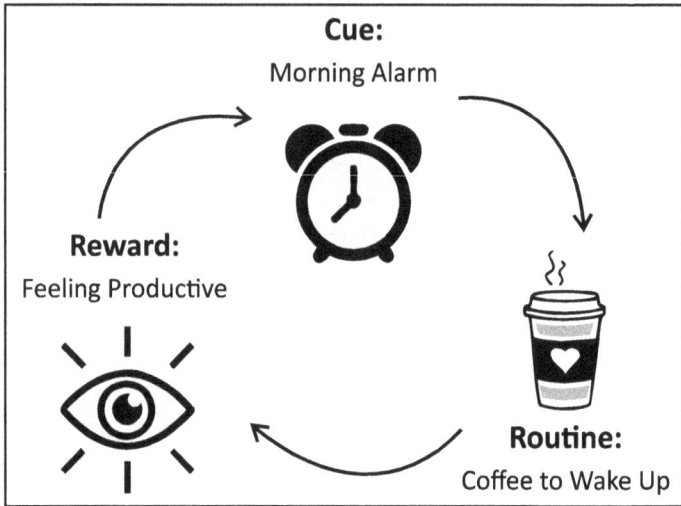

Cue:
Morning Alarm

Reward:
Feeling Productive

Routine:
Coffee to Wake Up

FUN FACT The "dopamine effect" of rewards explains why loyalty programs work. Brands like Starbucks and Sephora keep customers engaged by rewarding repeated purchases, triggering a subconscious habit loop (Duhigg, 2012).

5.3.2 Subconscious cues and cognitive biases

We like to think we're logical shoppers, but our brains rely on "cognitive biases"—mental shortcuts that help us make quick decisions. A few common biases, shown in Table 5.2, include anchoring bias, confirmation bias, and mere-exposure effect.

Table 5.2	Cognitive biases

Bias	Definition	Brand-related example
Anchoring	The first number or piece of information we see, like a "strikethrough" price, strongly influences our perception of value. This type of bias relies heavily on the first piece of information seen.	Showing an inflated "list price" so a discount seems more appealing
Confirmation Bias	Confirmation bias involves seeking information that upholds one's prior beliefs or impressions, ignoring contradictory information.	Noticing only brand cues that match a brand's 'premium' reputation
Mere-Exposure Effect	The tendency to develop a preference for something merely because it's familiar. When we repeatedly see a brand or slogan, we tend to favor it, even if we don't realize why.	Repetitive brand jingles make consumers more comfortable with that brand

Source: Adapted from Kahneman, 2011 & Thaler & Sunstein, 2008

Brands can use these insights to create smoother, more intuitive interactions, but there's a thin line between a helpful "nudge" and manipulation. Being transparent about discounts, clarifying fees, or using mere-exposure responsibly, rather than bombarding people with ads, fosters trust rather than undermining it.

Sensory cues

Beyond sight or logic, other senses can have a powerful sway. A distinct store scent, for instance, might instantly establish warmth and comfort before even a single product is seen. One example is a coffee shop that underscores its identity with the aroma of freshly ground beans, appealing to customers' subconscious desire for cozy familiarity.

Similarly, a well-crafted jingle or melody can stir emotional recall, forging direct links to the brand in a consumer's mind. These subtle tools amplify the emotional hook by tapping into deeper, automatic layers of perception, as discussed in Section 5.1, "The Role of Emotions in Brand Management."

Building ethical subconscious signals

Although subconscious cues can boost brand recall, they also bring ethical responsibilities. Brands that leverage background music to create a relaxed environment generally appear benign, but using overly aggressive lighting schemes or constant "FOMO" alerts can come off as manipulative.

Rather than subverting consumer autonomy, ethical brand managers aim to enhance the customer experience. For instance, offering a gentle product scent or clear signposting in a store fosters comfort without deceiving or pressuring the buyer.

5.3.3 Ethical neuromarketing

Neuromarketing techniques can be powerful, but they also raise ethical concerns (Murphy, Illes, & Reiner, 2008). Gathering brain-imaging data without clear consent or deliberately provoking fear erodes consumer trust. Instead, effective neuromarketing should strive to enhance experiences, like creating welcoming scents in a store or simplifying checkout flows, without trapping or misleading customers.

Maintaining consumer trust

Upholding trust involves clear communication around why and how subconscious cues are used. An online retailer that highlights "most popular" or "best value" products offers a helpful nudge, so long as the data are genuine. By contrast, "dark patterns" — where websites hide shipping fees or complicate cancellations — violate trust and can push customers away for good. Over time, repeated incidences of such manipulative techniques erode brand credibility, undoing any short-term gains they might produce.

> **POINT TO REMEMBER** Ethical branding isn't just about avoiding deception; it's about fostering long-term relationships where consumers feel respected and valued.

Blending innovation with responsibility

Advances in neuroscience offer exciting avenues to shape memorable brand experiences, through store layout innovations or personalized recommendations. Yet brand managers should merge these insights with empathy for users' well-being.

Frictionless purchasing flows and satisfying sensory elements enrich consumer satisfaction, provided they do not mislead or pressure. In other words, the best neuromarketing strategies guide customers rather than trick them. They enhance loyalty without compromising brand integrity.

Neuroscience offers a closer look at the subconscious processes shaping consumer decisions, from dopamine-driven habit loops that encourage repeat engagement to cognitive biases that color our perceptions (Plassmann et al., 2010). While these mechanisms often unfold behind the scenes, brand managers who acknowledge them can refine consumer experiences to be more intuitive and rewarding.

Tactics like selective attention and priming (Section 5.1.2) gain even greater traction when combined with deeper neuro-based insights, such as anchoring biases or sensory triggers.

However, this scientific toolkit for brand management must be used thoughtfully. Transparency about how a brand employs subtle cues, a commitment to respecting customer autonomy, and the avoidance of manipulative tactics help preserve trust in the long run. When these conditions are met, neuroscience-focused strategies can elevate engagement, nurture loyalty, and enhance brand perception, without compromising ethical standards.

5.4 Influencing Consumer Decision-Making

Winning customers isn't just about explaining product features. Modern consumers often let emotion, peer recommendations, and gut feeling guide them (Cialdini, 2007). We've discussed how trust, emotional triggers, and subconscious factors come into play in brand management. Now, let's see how brand managers can steer those decisions in ways that feel both persuasive and respectful.

5.4.1 Choice architecture

Choice architecture describes how options are presented, influencing what people choose (Thaler & Sunstein, 2008). Picture a grocery store placing fresh fruits at eye level to encourage healthier buys. In the case of online stores, it may look like highlighting the "best value" plan by default.

As long as you're open about your reasoning and don't hide alternatives, choice architecture can help customers navigate decisions more easily.

Nudges vs. Pushes: A nudge gently prompts beneficial behavior like defaulting to eco-friendly shipping, but still lets people opt out. On the other hand, heavy-handed tactics can backfire, damaging trust in the long run. For example, "pushes" can seem like forcing customers to jump through hoops to find a more budget-friendly plan.

As illustrated in Figure 5.3, subscription plans commonly use choice architecture by highlighting the best value option with flashy graphics and larger text.

Figure 5.3 Choice architecture

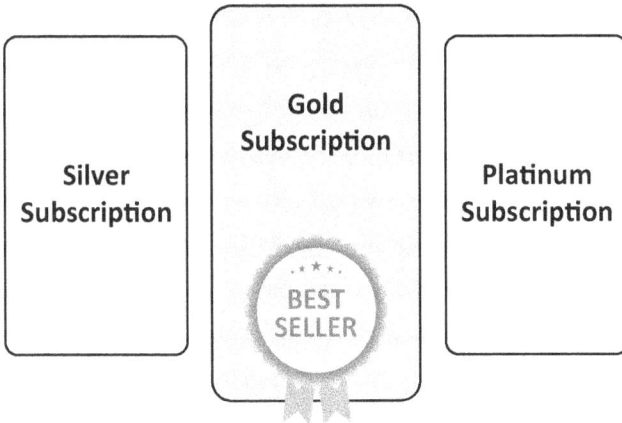

Silver
Subscription

Gold
Subscription

★ ★ ★
BEST
SELLER

Platinum
Subscription

FUN FACT Supermarkets often pump the scent of baked goods into the air near their bakery section. This subtle nudge increases impulse buying by creating a comforting, nostalgic feeling (Lindstrom, 2010).

DISCUSSION

As a brand manager, what are some creative ways you could think of to implement choice architecture into your strategy?

Balancing clarity with freedom

Effective choice architecture walks a careful line: it aims to simplify decisions while respecting consumers' autonomy. Overly complicated layouts or forced paths can spark frustration, potentially undermining the trust established by consistent brand actions (Morgan & Hunt, 1994).

POINT TO REMEMBER

Whether online or offline, the goal is to make options easy for the customer to find and comprehend. In doing so, brand managers can guide preferences ethically rather than forcing people into a purchase.

5.4.2 Ethical persuasion vs. manipulation

Persuasion can be constructive if it honestly outlines the pros, cons, and costs. Offering clear explanations of product features gives consumers the knowledge they need to make well-informed decisions (Kotler & Keller, 2016). This strategy complements the earlier focus on transparency and reliability. It emphasizes that the brand respects the consumer's ability to judge relevance.

Manipulation arises when facts are distorted or pressure tactics are used to spur hasty decisions (Fournier, 1998). Examples of manipulation include hidden fees, countdown timers that misrepresent stock levels, or intentionally misleading product images. Though these methods might deliver a brief spike in conversions, they erode trust over time.

Keeping in mind the role of subconscious mechanisms discussed in the neuroscience section, unethical manipulation exploits rather than informs the consumer's mental shortcuts. It potentially generates long-term reputational damage.

Respecting consumers' autonomy

Ethical persuasion also means honoring an individual's choice to opt out or explore competitors. Providing fair return policies, disclaimers of potential drawbacks, or clarifications about total costs are ways to show respect for the consumer's decision process. By acknowledging that the consumer retains control, brands strengthen credibility. This enables them to forge deeper customer relationships that can outlast fleeting market trends.

DISCUSSION

Have you ever felt manipulated by a brand's marketing tactics? What specific strategies made you feel pressured, and how did it impact your trust in that brand?

Chapter Summary

- Effective branding combines creativity with an understanding of how people process and remember information, both consciously and below awareness.

- Subconscious processes such as selective attention and priming can guide impressions before consumers consciously weigh pros and cons.

- Emotions like nostalgia, belonging, and empathy often outweigh purely logical factors, creating deeper brand connections.

- Trust results from consistent actions, transparent communication, and ethical alignment between a brand's claims and real performance.

- Cognitive dissonance weakens loyalty when brand promises and actual experiences conflict.

- Neuroscience insights such as reward pathways, habit loops, and cognitive biases explain how repeated positive interactions foster habit-like loyalty.

- Authentic storytelling and genuine customer testimonials build emotional resonance, helping people visualize personal benefits.

- Ethical persuasion emphasizes transparent choice architecture and open communication rather than high-pressure sales or hidden fees.

- Data-informed strategy ensures brand actions address real customer needs, while creativity keeps content engaging and memorable.

- Respect for consumer autonomy underpins long-term loyalty; customers appreciate honest guidance and meaningful brand values.

Quiz

1. **Which statement best describes why emotions are crucial to brand selection?**
   a. Emotional triggers are irrelevant once the customer compares prices.
   b. Emotions often override logical product considerations.
   c. Emotional marketing is illegal in certain regions.
   d. Emotions only matter for luxury brands.

2. **Selective attention refers to:**
   a. A consumer's inability to recall brand names.
   b. The brand's deliberate choice to limit advertising.
   c. The human tendency to filter out stimuli that aren't relevant to current interests or needs.
   d. An automated process that ranks social media ads.

3. **In brand messaging, priming works by:**
   a. Distracting consumers from actual product features.
   b. Preparing consumers to perceive subsequent information in a certain light.
   c. Guaranteeing better product performance.
   d. Setting fixed prices before negotiations begin.

4. **Cognitive dissonance arises when:**
   a. A brand's actions align with its stated promises.
   b. Consumers encounter contradictory information about a brand they trust.
   c. Brand managers focus on creative campaigns alone.
   d. Social media engagement outperforms traditional ads.

5. **Which approach helps reduce cognitive dissonance and fosters trust?**

    a. Constantly changing brand slogans and visuals to appear novel.

    b. Featuring hidden fees to increase short-term sales.

    c. Ensuring brand claims match real-world experiences.

    d. Avoiding any mention of brand ethics or sustainability.

6. **Dopamine's role in brand interactions primarily involves:**

    a. Making consumers immune to competitor discounts

    b. Encouraging repeat engagement when interactions are pleasing

    c. Hindering the memory of negative brand experiences

    d. Eliminating the need for logical product comparisons

7. **The term "habit loop" includes all of the following components except:**

    a. Cue

    b. Attitude

    c. Routine

    d. Reward

8. Anchoring bias means consumers:
   a. Always prefer the brand they first bought
   b. Are unaffected by initial price impressions
   c. Rely heavily on the first piece of information they encounter
   d. Only respond to the brand's default shipping method

9. Confirmation bias leads people to:
   a. Reject any new brand information that supports prior beliefs
   b. Seek and remember details that reinforce their existing views
   c. Value brand promises more than actual performance
   d. Choose random products to avoid brand loyalty

10. An example of leveraging sensory triggers ethically would be:
    a. Using a harsh strobe light in stores to hasten purchases
    b. Flooding customers with loud alarm sounds to promote urgency
    c. Infusing a signature store scent that gently reminds visitors of the brand
    d. Concealing windows so customers lose track of time

Answers

1 – b	2 – c	3 – b	4 – b	5 – c
6 – b	7 – b	8 – c	9 – b	10 – c

CHAPTER 6

The Role of Experience in Branding

Key Learning Objectives

- Explain why customer experience is a critical differentiator in contemporary markets.
- Identify specific techniques for creating memorable brand interactions, from strategic touchpoint design to sensory triggers.
- Discuss how personalization and digital innovations reshape the brand-customer relationship, ensuring relevance and connection.
- Understand the ethical and practical considerations of using customer data for unique experiences.
- Learn methods to measure experience quality, refine offerings, and continually elevate brand perception in a dynamic landscape.

A brand experience does more than fulfill basic needs. It can feel exclusive or high-end without the product itself being luxury-priced. Luxury often depends on context—a tiny café can appear just as upscale to regulars as a designer boutique might to its elite shoppers. Seemingly minor details, like a friendly website greeting or the playlist in a store, all contribute to how customers perceive your brand.

When businesses (of any size) apply principles like personalization or a thoughtfully crafted atmosphere, they create an experience that stands out. These elements spark emotional connections and help customers view the brand as something more meaningful than a simple commodity.

After exploring the psychological and neuroscientific foundations of branding in the previous chapter, we now focus on how these insights inform actual customer interactions. Understanding how consumers think and feel is a vital first step, but it is the execution of memorable experiences that secures a lasting place in their minds.

In this chapter, we will examine each point of contact, from initial marketing messages to follow-up services after a purchase. We will see how these aspects can evolve into meaningful touchpoints that drive loyalty. As you progress, you will uncover what it takes for a business to convert everyday encounters into experiences that resonate on a deeper level.

6.1 The Importance of Customer Experience in Modern Markets

For a long time, companies focused mostly on product features or lower prices to get ahead. But in our current marketplace, those basic selling points rarely set a brand apart. Today, a powerful way to shine is by delivering a memorable experience. When businesses zero in on how customers feel and engage with every step of the process, they build deeper relationships and foster long-term loyalty.

6.1.1 The Experience Economy

The evolution from product-centric marketing to an emphasis on experiences is closely linked to the concept of the Experience Economy (Pine and Gilmore,1999).

In simple terms, the phenomenon of "Experience Economy" describes that consumers no longer look solely for the best specifications or the lowest cost. Consumers today seek memorable interactions that engage their emotions and sense of identity. This shift challenges brands to go beyond basic features and create environments, events, or services that resonate on a deeper level.

Example: Starbucks does not simply sell coffee. Rather, it promotes a cozy atmosphere that invites customers to stick around. The décor, music, and even the drink-making process combine to form an experience unlike a typical coffee shop. This ambience goes beyond the product itself, reinforcing Starbucks' loyal fan base, even amid strong competition.

Table 6.1 below outlines the key differences between a product-focused and experience-focused brand approach.

Table 6.1	Product vs. Experience Approaches	
	Product-focused	**Experience-focused**
Core emphasis	Highlights features, specifications, or price advantages.	Creates emotional, memorable, and personalized connections with the brand to engage a sense of identity.
Marketing style	Stresses on utility and cost savings in campaigns.	Uses storytelling and immersive branding to deepen engagement.
Customer interaction	Typically transactional and brief.	Encourages community building, feedback, and extended customer involvement.
Example	"Our vacuum cleans 20% faster than competing models."	"Visit our interactive showroom for personalized demos and tips on how to get the best results from our vacuum."

By weaving emotional cues, consistent visuals, and genuine service into the customer journey, brands can create an experience that stands apart from competitors who rely solely on product features or price.

6.1.2 Consumer expectations in the Experience Economy

Thanks to social media and today's instant communication tools, people don't hesitate to talk about their brand encounters—good or bad. A single complaint, like an unhelpful service representative or a late delivery, can quickly undo a lot of the goodwill a brand has built up. In an age of instant sharing, stories can travel quickly; this pushes brands to deliver consistently great experiences at every turn.

To do this successfully, brand managers must outline which qualities matter most to their customers. Excelling in these key attributes shapes how buyers view the entire experience, typically resulting in deeper loyalty and repeat business.

> **TIP** Brand managers should consider how every detail, from store layout to online chat responses, reflects the brand's overarching story and values.

Table 6.2 outlines four key attributes that today's shoppers expect when engaging with a brand.

Table 6.2 **Key attributes consumers seek**

Key attribute	Explanation	Example
Efficiency and convenience	People value their time. Swift checkout processes, user-friendly websites, or easy appointment scheduling make interactions hassle-free.	An online retailer offering one-click checkout to reduce cart abandonment.
Personalized relevance	It refers to communication that addresses individual tastes or needs while using data ethically and without overstepping boundaries.	A streaming service that recommends shows based on past viewing history.
Emotional and social connection	Shoppers see brands as part of their identity. They look for shared values, community, and meaningful engagement.	A fitness brand that hosts online forums or local meet-ups for members.
Consistency and transparency	It means to have uniform standards across channels and clear policies on returns, data use, or sourcing.	A clothing label that openly shares its manufacturing practices.

Source: (Adapted from Pine & Gilmore, 1999 & Schmitt, 1999)

Understanding and implementing these attributes helps managers design strategies that align with customer expectations. In practical terms, each attribute represents a different layer in the "Consumer Expectations Pyramid" as illustrated in Figure 6.1 below. In this pyramid, the base layer is often speed and convenience, and higher layers encompass emotional bonds or ethical considerations.

Figure 6.1 **Consumer Expectations Pyramid**

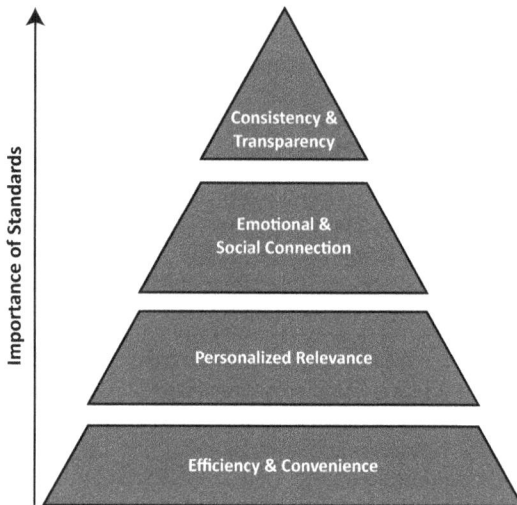

By recognizing the levels in this pyramid, businesses and brand managers can tailor their approach to meet, and eventually exceed, the standards that matter most to their audience.

6.1.3 Creating customer/brand experiences for competitive advantages

When multiple brands sell products at similar prices, it's often the customer experience that truly sets one apart. These experiences come from intangible factors like the company's culture, consistent visual themes, an upbeat staff, and even the music or aromas in a physical location. All of these touches work together to leave a lasting impression.

When these elements work together, they become difficult for competitors to replicate. This makes the overall experience of a brand a powerful differentiator. Table 6.3 provides examples of how each element can impact a brand's competitive advantage.

Table 6.3 Intangible elements of a brand experience

Element	How it builds advantage	Example
Company culture	Fosters employee pride and consistent brand values in every customer interaction.	A footwear company that trains all teams to deliver personal, empathetic support.
Design language	Conveys brand identity through visuals, packaging, and product aesthetics.	A technology brand that uses minimalist design to signal simplicity and elegance.
Staff attitude	Shapes consumer impressions through friendliness, expertise, and proactive service.	A luxury hotel chain with employees empowered to anticipate guest needs.
Ambience and senses	Creates an emotional connection by engaging sight, sound, smell, or touch.	A skincare boutique that uses subtle fragrance and soft lighting to relax visitors.

Businesses can apply these insights by auditing each element of the customer journey. For instance, managers might update store design to match new product lines or train staff to anticipate specific client preferences. These deliberate choices, when combined, produce memorable experiences that competitors struggle to imitate, paving the way for deeper loyalty.

Example: While Apple sells devices, it also curates a cohesive environment: minimalist retail spaces, intuitive interfaces, and consistent product aesthetics. This experience inspires brand devotion because fans feel part of a lifestyle, not just owners of a device.

> **POINT TO REMEMBER**
> Experience can be your most enduring competitive advantage. By unifying company culture, design, staff attitude, and environmental factors, you can deliver a powerful impression that outlasts price-based competition.

> **DISCUSSION**
> Recall a brand that you consider exceptional in terms of experience. Which intangible elements play the biggest role in making that experience stand out for you?

6.2 Creating Memorable Brand Experiences

Making a brand experience truly unforgettable means paying attention to each customer interaction, from the moment they first hear about you to the time they've used your product for weeks.

In Chapter 5, we discussed why it's so important to stand out emotionally and give people immersive moments. Now, let's translate those ideas into real-world tactics that managers can apply right away.

6.2.1 Sensory triggers and emotional hooks

To create memorable brand experiences, it is essential to engage the senses and tap into consumers' emotions. In this section, we provide a definitive list of sensory triggers, explaining how each sense plays a role in reinforcing brand identity. In addition, we explore emotional hooks that make experiences resonate on a deeper level.

1. Sensory triggers

According to Lindstrom (2010), engaging multiple senses plays a huge role in helping people recall and emotionally bond with a brand. By actively incorporating sight, sound, smell, touch, and even taste, marketers can design encounters that stick in customers' minds.

- **Sight:** A harmonious color palette, striking visuals, and a distinctive logo make your brand instantly recognizable. For example, a retailer that repeats the same unique color palette across its stores, website, and packaging becomes identifiable at a glance.
- **Sound:** A playful jingle or custom notification chime can spark memories and help to build emotional ties with your audience. A café that always streams its curated playlist effectively turns that soundtrack into a sonic logo for the brand.
- **Smell:** A specific fragrance in a store or lobby can bring back positive memories and set the right mood. Boutique hotels, for example, often diffuse a signature

scent in their lobbies to evoke an immediate sense of luxury and familiarity.

- **Touch:** Quality materials—whether in product packaging or décor—give people a tangible way to sense your brand's character. Consider a tech company that uses soft-touch materials for its product casings to underscore premium craftsmanship.

- **Taste:** For food brands, taste is obvious. But even non-food companies can incorporate tasting events or sponsor local food pop-ups to add another dimension to the experience. A gourmet food brand that hosts in-store tasting events lets customers sample the full range and connect flavor directly to brand perception.

2. Emotional hooks

While sensory cues help customers remember your brand, it's the emotional spark that truly forges a deeper bond. By weaving in compelling stories, personal conversations, and activities that foster a sense of community, brands can turn casual shoppers into committed advocates.

For example, highlighting genuine success stories or heartfelt testimonials allows people to imagine themselves as part of the brand's narrative, strengthening their emotional tie. Consider a fitness brand that shares member transformation stories and celebrates milestones publicly. This helps cultivate a sense of belonging and mutual encouragement.

> Think of a time when a sensory detail made a brand experience unforgettable for you. What was the trigger, and how did it shape your overall perception of the brand?

6.2.2 Designing consumer touchpoints

A "customer touchpoint" is any moment when a consumer interacts with a brand, whether online, in-store, or through any other channel.

To see the entire path customers take, brands often resort to "customer journey mapping" (Lemon & Verhoef, 2016). This approach reveals every interaction a buyer has with a brand. While the customer journey may vary depending on a brand's unique business model and offering, a standard customer journey can generally be broken into five main stages:

1. **Discovery:** Shoppers first hear about the brand through ads, social media buzz, or word-of-mouth.

2. **Consideration/ engagement:** They dig deeper, comparing choices or chatting with representatives for details.

3. **Purchase/ onboarding:** At the checkout stage, they receive any needed support to smoothly adopt or set up their new product.

4. **Usage/ support:** After buying, customers might reach out for help, get updates, or receive tips on how to maximize what they've purchased.

5. **Advocacy/ retention:** Delighted users often share good experiences with friends or online communities, effectively becoming brand ambassadors.

Mapping the journey in this way gives managers clear insights into where improvements can be made. They can also ensure that each stage stays aligned with the brand's values.

Figure 6.2 The customer journey

Every touchpoint matters. Consistently positive interactions across all touchpoints lead to a cumulative, memorable customer experience.

6.2.3 Types of consumers and their experiential needs

After mapping the customer journey, brand managers know *when* and *where* people interact with the brand. The next question is *who* those people are and *what* motivates them at each touch-point.

Table 6.4 outlines four core consumer types, highlighting the primary motivators that shape their behavior along the journey.

Table 6.4 Types of consumers

Consumer Type	Description	Example
Practical consumers	Value efficiency and functionality in every interaction	Shoppers who prioritize convenience over brand narrative
Experience seekers	Look for memorable, emotionally engaging encounters	Customers who return for the ambiance and personalized service
Conspicuous consumers	Place a high value on exclusive offerings and status symbols	Buyers attracted to limited-edition releases and premium events
Loyal advocates	Connect deeply with the brand story and actively share their experiences	Fans who recommend the brand through social media and word-of-mouth

Source: (Vigneron & Johnson, 1999)

Recognising which type of consumer you're addressing at a given stage helps you pick the right message, tone, and emotional lever. Weaving these insights into your brand's stories allows you to design experiences that stay true to your core values while making each customer feel seen and appreciated.

6.2.4 Storytelling in the physical or digital environment

Remember from earlier discussions that storytelling is a powerful tool in brand experience. Narratives give meaning to everyday interactions and help consumers relate to a brand on a personal level.

Simple storytelling can make everyday brand interactions feel meaningful. A small bookstore, for instance, could share personalized staff picks that explain why a certain title spoke to them. That way, customers feel like they're part of a cozy reading community. A warm layout, a few comfy chairs, and just the right music add to the story of exploration and belonging.

Online, an app might welcome users by name. It may assist them by keeping track of their fitness milestones and marking each success as part of their personal journey. These narrative touches help to build a real bond with the brand.

Brands should ask themselves questions such as:

- What is our unique selling point?
- What sets us apart from competitors?
- How can we translate our core values into a narrative that resonates with customers?

These prompts help in crafting a story that elevates the overall consumer experience.

The power of micro-moments

Micro-moments are brief but pivotal interactions like receiving a "thank you" confirmation email, a loyalty reward pop-up, or a personal note from a brand manager. Though tiny in isolation, these micro-moments accumulate, shaping overall impressions across various customer contact points.

A brand consistently delivering thoughtful micro-moments weaves a compelling "story in motion" that outperforms a single grand gesture. It reflects brand values and voice, and reinforces the overall story that a brand is telling.

Example: When a customer enters a high-end clothing store, their experience is enhanced by personalized greetings. Thoughtful product displays and staff who share insights into the brand's design philosophy improve satisfaction levels. This experience can trigger the customer's ideal self-image, making them feel confident and distinguished.

Storytelling can also tap into "conspicuous consumption." Here, buyers choose certain products to elevate their social standing (Veblen, 1899). Conspicuous consumption refers to purchasing products not only for their inherent utility but also to signal social status and personal success.

By emphasizing rare or premium aspects of your brand, you'll catch the eye of status-driven shoppers. This might include unveiling limited-edition product lines or hosting exclusive gatherings that pay tribute to your company's heritage. Such products are perfect for those who love to flaunt something unique.

6.3 Personalized and Unique Experiences in a Digital World

Today's buyers want a customized experience—even on the internet. Brands now have more data than ever on consumer preferences. However, the real trick is using that information thoughtfully to shape each customer's path. When executed well, personalization ensures customers feel genuinely appreciated, encouraging them to return time and again.

6.3.1 Personalized experience methods

Brands can adopt different methods to create experiences tailored to each customer. A travel website might offer personalized itinerary suggestions based on past trips. Or a beauty brand could send customized product recommendations. These methods enhance the customer experience and build lasting loyalty.

> **TIP** Businesses should continuously test and refine personalized strategies. Small adjustments based on customer feedback can lead to significant improvements in engagement and satisfaction.

Big data for personalization

"Big data" refers to the large volumes of information generated by digital interactions, from browsing behavior to purchase history. Today's digital world provides access to vast amounts of customer data, letting brands customize each step of the user journey like never before. Here are some ways data can drive personalization:

- **Preference tracking:** Noticing which pages people visit or how long they linger on a particular product helps brands offer suggestions that actually match their interests.

- **Predictive analysis:** Algorithms can guess what customers might need next by looking at their past behavior. This allows them to make recommendations that feel timely and relevant.

- **Automated segmentation:** Sorting shoppers into detailed groups, based on shared traits or habits, allows marketers to create messages that resonate better with each segment.

Gaining permission for data usage is paramount. Brands that hide extensive data collection behind complicated terms or rely on ambiguous "implied consent" risk reputational damage if customers feel deceived. Clear, user-friendly privacy statements, simple opt-outs, and transparent data-sharing policies not only comply with ethical standards but also build trust.

Effective personalization rests on four key practices: data collection, segmentation, notification, and transparency. The following table outlines recommended actions for each practice along with common pitfalls to avoid.

Table 6.5 Personalization do's and don'ts

Practice	Recommended action (Do)	Avoid (Don't)
Data collection	Clearly inform users and obtain consent.	Collect sensitive information without explanation.
Segmentation	Group customers by relevant, respectful criteria.	Use stereotypes or overgeneralize sensitive data.
Notification	Offer easy opt-outs and preference centers.	Send repeated or aggressive push notifications.
Transparency	Explain data usage in plain language.	Hide disclaimers in lengthy terms and conditions section.

POINT TO REMEMBER

Transparency and respect for customer privacy are key. A brand that communicates openly about its data practices will foster a more trusting relationship with its customers.

DISCUSSION

Think about a time when you received personalized recommendations from a brand. How did it affect your perception of that brand? What could have been done to make that experience even better?

6.3.2 Hybrid online-offline journeys

Personalization does not end with online interactions. A brand that integrates data-driven insights into real-world encounters ensures continuity at every touchpoint. For example, store associates who can access a customer's online profile may instantly see past purchases or preferred styles. This not only saves time but also creates a sense of seamlessness that elevates the overall brand experience.

Below are a few practical ways to bridge digital and physical channels:

- **In-store tablets or Augmented Reality (AR) displays:** Staff can check inventory in real time, show product variations with AR, or tailor suggestions based on a shopper's profile.

- **Click-and-collect models:** Customers order online and pick up items in person. This combines the convenience of digital shopping with the immediate gratification of examining goods in-store.

- **Virtual engagement:** In-person events, such as workshops or demos, can be livestreamed on social media. This allows remote viewers to interact, then later visit a physical location for follow-up activities.

The goal is not to duplicate every online feature in a physical space (or vice versa) but to make each channel play to its strengths. This holistic approach enhances personalization by letting customers experience the brand story no matter where they engage.

6.4 Elevating Your Brand Perception

We've talked a lot about giving current customers amazing experiences. But it's equally important to think about how everyone else, including potential buyers or onlookers, views your brand. In many ways, the way a brand is perceived becomes part of how loyal shoppers see themselves. If your brand symbolizes a particular attitude or lifestyle, your fans start to adopt that image too.

This idea links to the concept of an "ideal self." Many of us buy items that match how we want to appear—both to others and to ourselves. When a brand conveys qualities such as innovation, high-end appeal, or community spirit, it helps customers feel like they embody those traits too.

Example: Consider a sneaker brand known for street culture credibility. Even if someone does not currently own a pair, they may still view the brand as edgy or fashion-forward. Current users often gain social currency by wearing this brand. It affects how they feel about themselves and how others perceive them.

6.4.1 Practical tools for brand managers

Below is a straightforward checklist of concepts that businesses can use when designing brand perception strategies:

1. **Key brand qualities**
   - **Ask:** Which traits define our brand?
   - **Example answers:** Casual, sustainable, premium, friendly, professional

2. **Target audience perception**

   - **Ask:** How do we want both customers and non-customers to view the brand?

   - **Example answers:** As a trusted partner, as a cutting-edge innovator, or as a lifestyle brand

3. **Alignment with the ideal self**

   - **Ask:** How do these qualities fulfill a consumer's desired self-image?

   - **Example answers:** Using an eco-friendly line signals social responsibility, wearing our product conveys athletic prowess

4. **Communication channels**

   - **Ask:** Which forums (social media, in-store events, influencer partnerships) should we use to shape perception?

   - **Example answers:** Collaborate with eco-friendly influencers, host pop-up shops that highlight product origins

5. **Measuring perception**

   - **Ask:** How will we collect data on how people see the brand?

   - **Example answers:** Surveys, social listening, focus groups, net promoter scores

The Net Promoter Score (NPS) is an essential metric to gauge customer satisfaction in brand management. Let's understand how it works in the next sub-section.

6.4.2 Net Promoter Score

NPS is a measure of customer satisfaction that acts as a quick way to gauge brand loyalty (Reichheld, 2003).

Why does NPS matter for brand managers?

NPS refines customer sentiment into a single, trackable figure that can be benchmarked over time or compared with competitors. Because it ties directly to referral intent, it flags where to focus resources, whether that be on improving loyalty or furthering advocacy. Used regularly, NPS helps brand managers decide when to repair, refine, or simply reinforce the customer experience.

To determine the net promoter score, brand managers can ask a group of customers: *"On a scale of 1-100, how likely are you to recommend our brand to a friend or colleague?"* Score results fall into three categories:

- **Score 9-10**: Promoter (loves the brand, would spread the word)
- **Score 7-8**: Passive (happy but not enthusiastic)
- **Score 0-6**: Detractors (unhappy, may discourage others)

To calculate the NPS, follow these steps:

1. Determine what percent of the responses are promoter scores out of the total amount.
2. Determine what percent of the responses are detractor scores out of the total amount.
3. Subtract the percent of detractor scores from the percent of promoter scores

Net Promoter Score (NPS) = (%Promoter) - (%Detractor)

The outcome will be a number from -100 to +100. Any result above 0 is considered positive, while scores of 50 or more signify great word-of-mouth momentum.

Example: A brand manager surveys 200 customers and receives the following results: 110 gave 9–10 (Promoters), 60 gave 7–8 (Passives), and 30 gave 0–6 (Detractors).

- % Promoters = 110 / 200 = 55 %
- % Detractors = 30 / 200 = 15 %
- NPS = 55 – 15 = +40

In this case, the score of +40 tells the brand manager that the brand has solid advocacy (ie, more promoters than detractors) but there is still room to improve loyalty and convert passive customers into promoters.

6.4.3 Elements contributing to brand perception

Certain factors play a crucial role in how both customers and non-customers see a brand. These may include:

- **Visibility:** How often does the brand appear in relevant conversations or media?
- **Consistency:** Are the brand's tone and message the same in every channel?
- **Word of mouth:** What are people saying about the brand's value, service, or reputation?
- **Credibility:** Has the brand established trust through transparent practices or proven expertise?

Make sure each element reflects the same brand story. Disjointed messaging confuses audiences and weakens perception.

Designing strong experiences is an ongoing cycle of gathering feedback, refining your tactics, and staying innovative. Every improvement you make helps the brand remain relevant and competitive. Tracking perception among both customers and non-customers reveals how well you are connecting with your target audience. If you see a gap between how you want to be viewed and what people actually think, it is an opportunity to realign your brand story and customer interactions.

Brand perception and customer experience work together: a compelling perception can attract new consumers; similarly, a positive experience for existing buyers can strengthen that external image. By continuing to measure, adjust, and innovate, you build lasting equity and become the brand that people respect, trust, and aspire to engage with.

Use the knowledge from previous sections on emotional cues, storytelling, and personalization. Integrate these ideas into every customer-facing channel so that people outside your current customer base form a cohesive impression of what your brand represents.

6.4.4 Measuring experience quality and impact

Delivering a memorable brand experience is an ongoing effort. Managers need accurate ways to gather feedback, identify areas of opportunity, and continuously improve. The following tools and methods can help:

1. **Transactional surveys**

   Immediately after a purchase or customer service interaction, an automated survey such as NPS can gauge satisfaction. This quick check provides real-time insights on whether the experience met expectations.

2. **Focus groups**

   These groups include small, representative panels that discuss the brand's atmosphere, packaging, or service quality. Focus group sessions offer deeper insights into emotional responses. However, they can be time-intensive to organize.

3. **Mystery shopping**

   Trained evaluators act as regular customers, providing firsthand observations on everything from staff knowledge to cleanliness. While realistic, it represents only a snapshot of the customer journey.

4. **Social listening and sentiment analysis**

   By monitoring social media platforms, forums, and reviews, brands can track public sentiment and spot emerging trends or areas of concern.

| Table 6.6 | Methods for experience measurement |

Method	What it measures	Pros	Cons
Transactional surveys	Customer sentiment and likelihood of recommendation	Quick and simple to administer, recognized benchmark	Lacks explanation of the reason behind responses
Focus groups	In-depth qualitative feedback	Reveals deeper emotional cues, brand perceptions	Time-consuming, could lead to potential bias if not well-run
Mystery shopping	Realistic, on-the-ground brand experience check	Helps evaluate staff performance, brand alignment	Limited sample, may not reflect a typical customer
Social listening	Organic opinions from public forums/ social media	Broad scope, can spot unexpected trends	Requires robust analysis tools, can be scattered

Bringing together feedback from multiple sources paints a comprehensive picture of how customers experience the brand. Once managers see what works and what does not, they can begin refining the brand experience through a cycle of small yet meaningful adjustments, such as:

- **User flow redesign:** Streamlining an e-commerce checkout page to reduce cart abandonment
- **Localized partnerships:** Collaborating with local artisans for limited-edition items that reflect regional culture
- **Community-building updates:** Launching in-app forums or newsletters that invite loyal customers to share feedback or beta-test new features

The methods outlined in Table 6.6 above are most powerful when they feed on an ongoing loop of improvement. Figure 6.3 illustrates a five-step cycle: collect feedback, identify pain points, make changes, measure results, and repeat. Running through this loop ensures that every insight a brand manager gathers will translate into concrete upgrades to the customer experience and, ultimately, to the brand perception you set out to shape.

Figure 6.3 Iterative improvement cycle

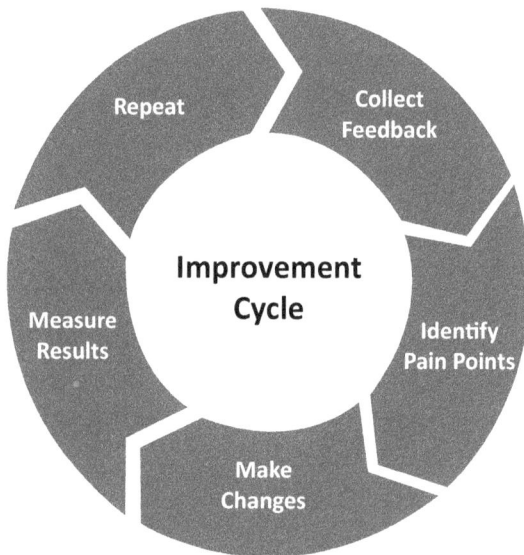

Gathering feedback, spotting problems, and improving each phase of the customer experience isn't something you do just once. It's an ongoing loop that helps your brand stay fresh and in tune with shifting trends and customer demands. By constantly fine-tuning, you'll remain one step ahead in a market that never stands still.

Throughout this chapter, we examined how experiences create lasting impressions. They enhance loyalty and set the stage for authentic brand advocacy. By combining emotional cues, personalized engagement, and well-defined customer touchpoints, managers can position their brands for sustained success. In the next chapter, we will explore strategies for effective brand communications and marketing. We shall focus on how to share these experiences and stories with a broader audience.

Chapter Summary

- The Experience Economy shifts brand focus from product features to holistic customer engagement, making customer experience a primary differentiator.

- Consumers expect efficiency, convenience, and emotional resonance across all touchpoints.

- Emotional connections create intangible assets, transforming simple shoppers into advocates who share positive brand stories.

- Sensory triggers and narrative-driven encounters deepen brand impressions. They turn ordinary transactions into memorable moments.

- Consistent emotional cues, thoughtful support, and personal touches combine to forge strong, enduring loyalty.

- Touchpoint design spans the entire journey—from awareness to advocacy—so that each step reinforces brand values and eliminates friction.

- Personalization leverages data to deliver tailored experiences. However, it must respect user privacy and autonomy to maintain credibility.

- Bridging digital and in-person channels (e.g., click-and-collect, in-store tablets) offers seamless transitions that enrich the overall customer journey.

- Ongoing measurement of customer experience relies on feedback loops through tools such as NPS, surveys, and social listening. These tools identify issues early and guide iterative enhancements.

- A cycle of designing, evaluating, and refining brand interactions sustains relevance in evolving marketplaces where experiences trump product specifications.

- Incremental updates, such as refining user flows or adding region-specific elements, show an ongoing commitment to consumer needs.

- By publicizing improvements, like sustainable packaging or better loyalty perks, brands reveal behind-the-scenes care, reinforcing trust.

- In the long term, a brand's "signature experience" stands out among competitors. It becomes a durable source of differentiation and brand equity.

Quiz

1. **Which of the following best captures the shift from product-focused marketing to experience-focused marketing?**
   a. Eliminating emotional appeals to emphasize facts
   b. Stressing purely logistical details in all promotional materials
   c. Highlighting holistic engagement and consumer emotions beyond mere product specifications
   d. Focusing on the cheapest option available to attract price-sensitive shoppers

2. **Why do intangible brand experiences often offer a stronger competitive edge than price or features?**
   a. Experiences are easily replicated by rivals.
   b. Experiences become part of a deeply rooted emotional bond that is harder to duplicate.
   c. Low prices always attract more loyalty.
   d. Consumers only remember brand logos, not service quality.

3. **In an experience-driven marketplace, negative feedback from a single bad encounter can:**
   a. Have minimal impact on modern social media channels
   b. Potentially overshadow a long history of positive interactions
   c. Always guarantee an automatic drop in brand equity
   d. Remain invisible if the brand invests enough in conventional ads

4. Which factor is typically not considered a core element of a powerful brand experience?
   a. Emotional resonance
   b. Low operational costs for the brand
   c. Tailored messaging for each customer segment
   d. Consistency in brand tone and visuals

5. A brand that carefully orchestrates waiting areas, staff uniforms, and store layout is focusing on which concept?
   a. Digital transformation
   b. Sensory uniformity
   c. Environmental storytelling
   d. Pricing strategies

6. Which statement correctly describes "micro-moments"?
   a. Extended brand events lasting multiple hours
   b. Tiny interactions like confirmation emails or quick product demos that subtly reinforce brand perception
   c. Areas where brand messages must be strictly logical
   d. Stages in the brand life-cycle that ignore consumer feedback

7. Sensory triggers aid brand recall because:
   a. They only appeal to consumers who ignore text-based marketing.
   b. Engaging multiple senses can produce stronger, more lasting mental associations.
   c. Consumers always prefer loud music or overpowering scents.
   d. Government regulations mandate the use of distinct scents for brand compliance.

8. **Why is narrative an effective technique in brand experiences?**

    a. It replaces the need for functional product details.

    b. Stories invite consumers to see themselves in the brand's journey.

    c. A single anecdote can override consistent brand failures.

    d. Narratives always guarantee large advertising budgets.

9. **Which of the following best reflects an ethical approach to personalization?**

    a. Gathering personal data secretly and assuming consent

    b. Automatically signing up users for location-based notifications without an opt-out

    c. Providing users with clear control over which data is collected and how it's used

    d. Publishing user profiles publicly as a marketing tactic

10. **When integrating data insights into in-store interactions, a primary benefit is:**

    a. Prolonged wait times to encourage impulse buys

    b. Creating a fragmented brand journey across multiple channels

    c. A seamless connection between online browsing and offline shopping experiences

    d. Restricting brand access to specific age groups

Answers

1 – c	2 – b	3 – b	4 – b	5 – c
6 – b	7 – b	8 – b	9 – c	10 – c

CHAPTER 7

Brand Communications and Marketing

Key Learning Objectives

- Understand why consistent brand messages are vital across both online channels and traditional media.
- Explore brand equity and its relation to awareness, loyalty, and a cohesive brand identity.
- Discover ways to boost brand recognition through repeated cues, unique elements, and collaborations.
- Understand how peer endorsements and user-created content (UGC) influence how people view and trust your brand, helping you steer meaningful user interactions.
- Get familiar with proven techniques for guiding online communities and handling user posts in a responsible way, reinforcing trust and genuine interactions.

We've learned how well-crafted experiences can elevate a brand beyond simple product features and influence how the public sees it. Now it's time to look at the methods and platforms that share a brand's identity with a broader market.

Brand communications involve expressing a company's vision, mission, and values. Marketing covers the wider tactics that boost product visibility and grow brand equity. Working together, these efforts encourage awareness, interaction, and strong customer bonds.

Modern shoppers jump easily between social networks, video-streaming services, e-commerce sites, and brick-and-mortar stores. At every turn, they expect messages that line up and offer real value. Coming up, we'll dig into strategies for weaving brand equity across these different spaces. We'll also explore how endorsements from peers and community-led stories can deepen trust. Ultimately, effective communication and marketing reinforce the unique brand experiences designed by a business.

To guide these efforts, the Eight Ps of marketing (Lovelock & Wright, 2002), known as the Marketing Mix, offer an expanded framework that accommodates the complexities of modern brand marketing:

The Marketing Mix:

1. **Product:** The offerings and how they satisfy customer needs
2. **Price:** The cost strategy and perceived value
3. **Place:** Distribution channels or platforms used to reach customers
4. **Promotion:** The communication methods designed to inform or persuade
5. **People:** The individuals who represent and influence the brand, internally and externally
6. **Process:** The systems and workflows that maintain consistent quality

7. **Physical Evidence:** Tangible elements that signal brand promise, such as packaging or store design

8. **Partnerships:** Working with like-minded organizations or leveraging shared resources

The eight key areas of the marketing mix (Figure 7.1) work together like a well-oiled machine that guides a brand's marketing efforts. Using this mix, brand managers can organize a well-rounded communication and marketing plan, guaranteeing that every touchpoint upholds a strong, cohesive message.

Figure 7.1 The Marketing Mix

Source: (Adapted from Lovelock & Wright, 2002.)

7.1 Cross-Channel Consistency

Consider a typical consumer journey. An individual may first discover a brand on a podcast, explore its Instagram feed, visit the website for product details, and finally visit a physical store. Each step influences how they perceive the brand. If the tone or visuals differ drastically between these platforms, customers may find the brand's identity unclear or contradictory. Consistency across channels reinforces brand recognition, builds trust, and helps people quickly understand the brand's personality and values.

7.1.1 Aligning marketing and communication channels with the 8 Ps

Marketing and communication channels cover both online and offline platforms.

- **Online Channels:** Include websites, social media, email newsletters, and digital ads.
- **Offline Channels:** Might involve print media, television, radio, and physical retail spaces.

Although these channels differ in format, each one provides an opportunity to reflect the eight Ps of marketing and contribute to a cohesive brand image. Table 7.1 references how each of the eight Ps can translate into brand communications and influence consumer perception:

| Table 7.1 | The 8 Ps in Brand Communications |

Marketing 'P'	Application	Example
Product	Highlight product benefits and relevance to consumer needs	Online ads featuring key product features or in-store displays that let customers test items
Price	Convey pricing strategy and value proposition	Promotions emphasizing cost-effectiveness or luxury depending on the target audience
Place	Ensure visibility across online and offline retail channels	Coordinated e-commerce site, physical store layouts, and pop-up events in locations where customers congregate
Promotion	Use targeted campaigns and messaging to reach the audience	Consistent branding across social media, email marketing, direct mail, and in-store signage
People	Showcase brand representatives and customer service ethos	Trained customer support staff, influencer partnerships, or brand ambassadors who embody brand values
Process	Communicate operational efficiency and service reliability	Clear return policies, quick checkout procedures, and transparent timelines for shipping or service delivery
Physical Evidence	Provide tangible elements that reinforce the brand message	Thoughtful packaging, store décor, uniform branding in marketing materials, and distinct color schemes
Partnerships	Highlight collaborations that add value or expand reach	Co-branded products, shared promotions with complementary brands, or local community sponsorships

Source: (Adapted from Lovelock & Wright, 2002)

Balancing online and offline experiences is crucial, too. For example, if your social pages are fun and energetic, your retail space should mirror that vibe. Likewise, a physical location with a sleek and modern design should carry that same look onto your website and app. When every channel feels in

> **TIP** Before launching a new campaign or update, check how each channel will represent these Ps. Presenting yourself with a uniform style and voice helps customers form the same impression, no matter how they interact with your brand.

sync, people trust and appreciate the brand more—and they quickly pick up on its core values.

> **DISCUSSION** Choose a brand you interact with regularly. List the different online and offline touchpoints you use, and note whether the brand's communication style feels consistent across each channel. What could the brand do to improve consistency and reinforce its identity?

7.1.2 Unifying brand communications

When we talk about uniformity in communications and cross-channel consistency, we're really talking about giving people the same clear message, wherever they encounter your brand. But consistency doesn't mean boring. The key is to keep your style, tone, and values intact while adjusting each message to suit different platforms or audiences.

In bigger companies, siloed teams can undermine this goal. Without clear brand standards or open communication, groups like retail, public relations, and customer support may each shape the brand differently. Collaboration and well-defined brand guidelines help avoid those disconnects and maintain one united voice.

Brand managers can ensure consistency by establishing shared style guides, setting up cross-departmental planning sessions, and communicating core brand values at every level of the company.

Table 7.2 provides an overview of some of the most frequent obstacles brand managers have in unifying their brand communications, along with practical solutions.

Table 7.2 Cross-channel consistency challenges and solutions

Challenge	Description	Solution
Siloed teams	Different departments working with inconsistent guidelines	Develop a shared brand handbook and hold regular cross-team workshops
Inconsistent tone	Formal tone in email, casual on social media, unclear in print	Define a brand "voice" with personality traits that can adapt to context
Over-localization	Regional offices drift away from the core brand identity	Provide local flexibility but keep key brand attributes consistent
Rapid platform changes	Frequent emergence of new social channels	Maintain core brand pillars and adjust formats to suit platform needs

When everyone works together under the same guidelines, customers see one seamless brand story. This shared vision drives everything from new product rollouts to social media outreach. It ensures each interaction reflects the brand's identity.

7.1.3 Ensuring a cohesive brand voice and visual identity

Brand communications center on cohesive messaging and visuals that help people spot and connect with the organization.

- **Brand voice:** The overall style, tone, and personality woven into every channel.
- **Visual identity:** The design pieces that give a brand a consistent, memorable look.

When these two dimensions align, they reinforce each other and enhance brand perception. Consistency does not mean using the exact same language on every platform. Instead, the foundational tone or style remains stable while adapting to context.

Example: The same brand might strike a friendlier tone on social media and maintain a more formal one in a financial report. The key is ensuring the brand's core traits remain identifiable, regardless of the channel.

Connecting the eight Ps to brand voice and visual identity

Several of the eight Ps of marketing come into play when crafting a unified brand presentation. Product, Promotion, and Physical Evidence are particularly relevant:

- **Product:** Packaging design, product features, and naming conventions can reflect the brand's core style. For example, an organic cosmetics line with minimalist, eco-friendly packaging that matches a sustainability theme.
- **Promotion:** The brand would benefit from marketing campaigns, social media posts, and email newsletters that use a consistent voice and visuals. For example, a travel brand that creates ads with the same color palette and friendly, adventurous language.

- **Physical Evidence:** Store layouts, event booths, and printed materials all reinforce brand identity. For example, a tech retailer that uses a signature font and color scheme on signage, staff uniforms, and bags.

Aligning these aspects of the marketing mix with a clear voice and cohesive visuals helps consumers quickly understand and trust the brand message.

Ensuring that every promotional or product-related material follows brand guidelines can elevate the brand experience. Customers see familiar motifs, colors, and phrases that instantly remind them of the brand, building recognition and loyalty.

Practical tips for maintaining consistency:

1. **Create a central style guide:** Identify approved color codes, fonts, logos, and voice guidelines. This ensures that anyone producing content or designing materials works from the same core references.

2. **Adapt locally but stay true to the brand:** Some markets have cultural nuances. A brand might tweak color choices or imagery without losing its core identity. For instance, red may signify good fortune in certain regions.

3. **Encourage cross-departmental sharing:** Teams responsible for social media, retail displays, and packaging should collaborate or consult the same reference materials to stay aligned.

4. **Checklists and Review:** A basic checklist can catch inconsistencies before they reach consumers. For instance, does the design follow official color codes? Does the text match the defined brand voice?

Brand managers can use the following checklist to maintain consistency when crafting a campaign or updating a communications strategy.

Brand voice and visual identity checklist:

1. **Tone consistency**

   - Does the text reflect the overall personality and values of the brand?
   - Have you kept the same style of language across platforms, while allowing for slight variations in formality?

2. **Design elements**

   - Do logos, fonts, and color palettes match what is outlined in the style guide?
   - Are any regional adaptations made without losing the core brand look?

3. **Message clarity**

   - Is the main message conveyed in a way that fits the brand's existing campaigns?
   - Do all visual and textual components reinforce that message?

4. **Platform suitability**

   - Have you adjusted the content length or tone to suit the channel? For example, short-form video for TikTok vs. written blog posts?
   - Does each platform still feel like part of the same brand ecosystem?

5. **Final review**

   • Is the final piece consistent with previous materials, yet updated for context or market changes?

   • Have all relevant stakeholders or team leaders signed off on the final look and feel?

Unified voice and visuals signal professionalism and clarity, making it easier for customers to recognize the brand. By integrating the eight Ps into all communications and double-checking for consistency, brand managers can ensure that every touchpoint reflects a strong, memorable identity.

7.1.4 Integrating traditional and digital marketing

A cohesive brand message spans every point of contact, whether in person or online. While digital platforms may dominate today's landscape, traditional marketing (billboards, print ads, radio spots) still reaches large audiences.

Aligning these channels with the same brand voice and visual identity builds consumer trust and recognition. Creating synergy across offline and online methods enables brands to maximize their reach and showcase a consistent image.

1. **Traditional Marketing:** Provides advantages like tactile engagement and local targeting.

   Table 7.3 below offers examples of common traditional channels and how they can reflect brand identity.

Table 7.3 Traditional marketing channels

Traditional channel	Key features	How to reinforce brand identity
Billboards	High visibility, local influence	Use the same color palette and tagline as digital campaigns.
Print ads	Physical presence, design detail	Add a Quick Response (QR) code that leads to a landing page with matching design elements.
Radio spots	Memorable audio, repeated exposure	Maintain the same tone of voice heard in your videos or podcasts.
In-store displays	Direct brand immersion for customers	Use consistent fonts, colors, and logos that match social media posts.

2. **Digital Marketing:** Online platforms allow for real-time data, interactive formats, and broader reach. Table 7.4 highlights popular digital channels.

Table 7.4 Digital Marketing Channels

Digital Channel	Key features	How to reinforce brand identity
Social media	Rapid two-way interaction, user-generated content	Maintain a signature hashtag and brand tone that matches offline materials.
Web ads	Targeted reach, measurable conversions	Use consistent color schemes and Calls-to-Action (CTAs) that mirror print or billboard ads.

Digital Channel	Key features	How to reinforce brand identity
Email marketing	Personalized outreach, segmentation	Align the email design with brand fonts and imagery from brochures or packaging.
Video platforms	Engaging visuals, storytelling opportunities	Continue themes from TV commercials, using the same narrative style.

3. Hybrid campaigns

Some of the strongest marketing strategies merge traditional and digital channels. For instance, a television ad could end by inviting viewers to enter an online contest or check out a branded hashtag. This nudge moves them effortlessly from traditional media into digital engagement, carrying the brand story across different platforms.

4. Calls-to-Action (CTAs)

Print ads or billboards can integrate QR codes linking to a campaign page. Radio spots can include concise URLs that redirect to specific parts of a website. These features prevent any channel from existing in isolation, creating a larger brand ecosystem where each piece connects back to the same core message.

Figure 7.2	Billboard CTA

Source: QRCodeChimp.com

A CTA, such as a QR code, placed on a billboard successfully engages consumers with brands via traditional marketing outputs.

5. **Measuring impact across channels**

Brands can track digital traffic originating from offline ads by using unique codes, specialized web addresses, or dedicated phone numbers. Meanwhile, data from traditional campaigns, such as store visits or redeemed coupons, offers feedback on whether the overall marketing effort is effective. Insights from one channel can inform adjustments in the other, building a well-synchronized brand experience.

FUN FACT Social media is a top discovery channel for new brands, with 55% of American consumers learning about unfamiliar products there (Sprout Social, 2021).

6. Importance of placement and brand identity

Placement is not only about finding the right audience. It is about maintaining the integrity of the brand. An advertisement displayed in an inappropriate context can clash with the company's image. Whenever possible, select environments and partners that align with the brand's standards and aesthetic.

When brands merge old-school tactics with digital channels, they can reach diverse audiences while staying consistent. That way, whether someone's first impression is a print ad or a TikTok video, the message remains authentic, clear, and tied to the bigger strategy.

TIP Placement (the "Place" element of the marketing mix) is part of brand identity. An ad that appears in a setting with negative associations, for example, near a trash bin or questionable content, can create unwanted connotations. Choose locations that match the brand's values and messaging.

7.1.5 Global vs. localized communication

Brands with international footprints must juggle global consistency with local adaptability. A single voice across drastically different cultural contexts can appear tone-deaf. Conversely, a hyper-local approach might dilute brand identity if each region develops contradictory styles.

Example: Despite a globally recognized logo and color scheme, Coca-Cola regularly tailors campaigns to local festivities or traditions. These localized versions revolve around the same brand spirit (happiness, sharing) but adapt cultural references, languages, and imagery to connect authentically.

POINT TO REMEMBER Strive for a balance that respects local culture and remains true to the overarching brand promise. This approach strengthens global reach without losing the distinctive identity that defines the brand.

FUN FACT McDonald's "I'm Lovin' It" launched in 2003 and quickly became the chain's longest-running slogan worldwide (McDonald's Corporate Reports, 2003–2008). The simple three-word English tagline and five-note jingle were easy to translate, letting each market swap in local language, artists, and imagery while the core hook stayed intact, proving to be an ideal example of global consistency paired with local relevance.

7.2 Brand Equity and Recognition

Brand equity: The total worth a brand carries in the market, shaped by how people perceive it, the loyalty they show, and the associations they make beyond the product's core utility (Aaker, 1991).

Brands with strong equity can charge more, build dedicated communities, and more easily break into new product lines or markets.

7.2.1 Defining brand equity components

Various models break down brand equity into several complementary parts. One well-known framework is presented by Aaker (1991), which highlights five key elements that drive how customers perceive and remain loyal to a brand. These five elements work together to form the foundation of brand equity:

1. **Brand awareness:** This is the baseline: do people remember your brand name when a product category pops up? Solid awareness means you're automatically on shoppers' shortlists.

2. **Perceived quality:** It refers to the sense of overall reliability or prestige that consumers attach to your brand. People often spend more on items they consider trustworthy or high-end.

3. **Brand associations:** This involves any emotional or practical ideas customers connect to your brand. For instance, in the automobile segment, many see Jeep as adventurous, while Volvo is synonymous with safety.

4. **Brand loyalty:** It refers to how firmly customers stick with and recommend your brand, even when alternatives

pop up. This bond grows through consistent user experiences, thoughtful perks, or deep emotional connections.

5. **Other proprietary assets:** They include aspects like trademarks, patents, or exclusive distribution deals that keep rivals at a distance and safeguard your brand's unique market position.

If you see that one slice of your brand equity (like awareness or loyalty) lags behind, aim your marketing efforts right at that gap. Strengthening each component in turn helps elevate the brand's overall reputation.

DISCUSSION

Consider a brand you buy often. Which part of its equity—awareness, perceived quality, associations, loyalty, or unique assets—do you think truly distinguishes it, and why?

7.2.2 Building brand recognition

Achieving strong brand recognition means appearing across multiple channels while staying true to the brand's core identity. Distinctive elements such as jingles, slogans, and mascots serve as mental shortcuts that help consumers instantly identify the brand. Below are some practical steps for brand managers looking to increase brand recognition:

1. **Define distinctive brand assets:** Develop recognizable visuals like color schemes, logos, taglines, and audio cues that reinforce the brand's personality.

2. **Be consistent with messaging:** Use the same tone, style, and core themes across all platforms, from social media ads to product packaging.

3. **Use multiple channels for exposure:** Reach consumers where they spend their time. This can include digital ads, influencer collaborations, and even offline venues such as trade shows.

4. **Monitor and adapt:** Track which assets resonate best and refine your strategy based on data, market trends, and audience feedback.

A. Repetition and consistency

Frequent but consistent messaging cements brand attributes in consumer minds. For instance, McDonald's uses the golden arches and the "I'm Lovin' It" slogan across mediums. This ensures global audiences instantly recognize its identity.

B. Partnerships and sponsorships

Aligning with compatible events, charities, or influencers can accelerate recognition. For instance, when an outdoor apparel brand sponsors a major mountain-climbing event, it associates itself with adventure, natural exploration, and community.

Figure 7.3	Consistent branding

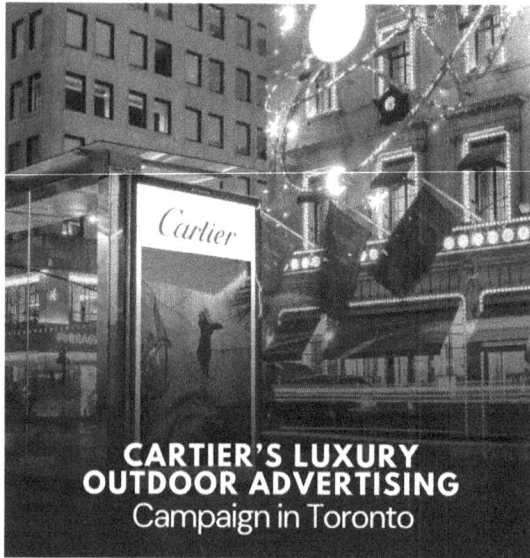

Source: (Zanni, 2024)

Luxury goods brand Cartier ran a strategically placed outdoor advertising campaign in Toronto, Canada. The locations aligned with the luxury brand image, such as on the high shopping street and outside a luxury hotel.

DISCUSSION

Think of a brand you encounter regularly. Which elements (logos, mascots, slogans, or specific sponsorships) contribute most to its recognizability? How do these elements appear across different channels?

7.2.3 Protecting and expanding equity

A strong brand can extend its influence into new product lines or markets, but such expansions must be carefully managed. In the context of the eight Ps of marketing, the "Product" is a pivotal element. Any new product offering must reflect the brand's core values and quality standards to preserve consumer trust.

Example: A footwear brand moving into the sports apparel segment can benefit from existing brand equity, yet a hasty launch of low-quality items might undermine the reputation built over time.

A. Brand extensions vs. Brand expansions

- **Brand extension:** Leveraging an established brand name to introduce new products or categories that align with the original positioning. An example might be a luxury fashion house releasing a fragrance line.

- **Brand expansion:** More broadly, this can encompass larger strategic moves like entering entirely new markets, acquiring complementary businesses, or significantly revising brand direction.

Below are three common types of extension strategies:

1. Line extensions

Creating sub-lines within the same business category. A perfume brand might add a line of luxury accessories under the same name. Maintaining quality across these sub-lines is essential to avoid weakening the main brand.

2. Geographic expansion

Moving into new regions requires cultural sensitivity. Brand managers may need to adapt certain features, messaging, or even color schemes while preserving fundamental brand DNA.

3. Rebranding or refreshing

Over time, logos, packaging, or color palettes can feel outdated. Small updates energize the brand's image, but drastic changes risk alienating loyal customers. Successful refreshes maintain recognizable elements for continuity.

B. Avoiding overextension

While extending a brand can open up new revenue streams and broaden its appeal, pushing too far or too fast can dilute hard-earned equity. Overextension happens when the new addition conflicts with the brand's core image or strains organizational resources.

Table 7.5 **Risks of brand overextension**

Risk	Description	Example
Brand dilution	Straying from core identity diminishes consumer trust	A luxury label releasing cheap items that clash with its premium image
Cannibalization	New lines undercut existing products or confuse positioning	A tech firm overshadowing its flagship line with multiple, similar offerings
Operational complexity	Overly ambitious scaling disrupts supply chain or operations	A fast-food chain venturing into unrelated merchandise, complicating logistics

Risk	Description	Example
Mixed consumer messages	Conflicting signals about brand direction or target audience	A sustainable brand offers a new product that uses an excessive amount of plastic packaging

By aligning each new initiative with the brand's existing equity and maintaining consistent quality, brand managers can protect the core identity and also reach new audiences.

7.2.4 Measuring brand equity

Monitoring brand equity is crucial for tracking the impact of marketing strategies. It also helps to spot early signs of decline. However, quantifying perceptions that exist largely in consumers' minds can be challenging. Let's explore four methods that can help gain tangible insights into a brand's standing:

1. **Consumer surveys**

   Ask about brand recognition, preference, and associations. This can include straightforward questions about which brands come to mind first in a category, or more detailed queries about perceived values, quality, and personality. The results offer direct feedback from the people whose opinions matter most.

2. **Price premium analysis**

   Compare your prices to those of similar competitors. If consumers are willing to pay more for your brand, it often signals higher perceived value. Track whether your brand can maintain or even increase this premium over time.

3. **Market share**

   Evaluate whether the brand holds a strong competitive position. Consistent or growing market share is usually a sign of robust equity, as customers choose your brand over alternatives. If market share dips, investigate possible declines in brand preference or an increase in strong rival brands.

4. **Financial valuation**

   Some companies project earnings or consider the future cash flow tied to the brand name. This might involve consulting with valuation experts. Such experts help to estimate how much the brand itself, separate from tangible assets, is worth.

   Regularly reviewing these metrics gives brand managers a clearer view of whether brand-building investments are paying off or if signs of brand equity erosion are starting to appear.

   While each metric has its limits, using multiple methods together can paint a well-rounded picture of brand equity. Balance direct consumer insights like surveys with market performance like price premiums and market share. This highlights strengths and addresses weaknesses.

7.3 Social Proof and User-Generated Content

   Consumers often trust peer opinions more than direct promotional messages. This makes social proof a key element of modern marketing. Recall from Section 5.2 of Chapter 5, "Word of mouth magic," that third-party validation can shape brand perceptions. By combining the power of community engagement with a consistent brand voice, managers can amplify positive impressions and nurture stronger customer relationships.

7.3.1 Leveraging social proof for credibility

Social Proof: The idea that people gauge an offering's value or relevance by observing others' behavior (Cialdini, 2007).

If numerous buyers praise a brand or product, new potential customers assume it must be good. Comments, reviews, and user-submitted posts often have more impact on public opinion than official ads. Platforms like Tripadvisor or Amazon can show star ratings and user endorsements that influence purchase decisions more than their own marketing claims.

Figure 7.4 Social proof in action on Shein

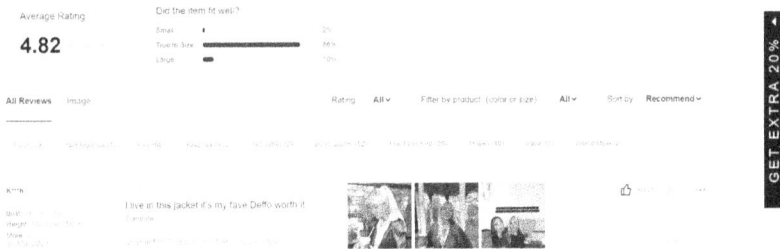

Source: (Chauhan, 2025)

Many e-commerce fashion brands social proof for credibility by building verified customer reviews and photos into the product page.

FUN FACT Over 80% of consumers trust recommendations from people they know above all other forms of advertising (Nielsen, 2021).

Common social proof elements

Social proof can appear in different forms, each reinforcing credibility from a slightly different angle. Below are three key elements that brand managers can harness to demonstrate quality and build trust:

A. Reviews and star ratings

Platforms like Amazon or Yelp reveal average user ratings. A high rating can dramatically boost conversions, while a low one deters prospective buyers.

B. Testimonials

Quoted endorsements from respected industry figures or everyday customers lend authenticity.

C. Influencer partnerships

Collaborating with personalities known for specific niches—like fitness, gaming, or fashion—can align a brand with the influencer's follower base, speeding brand acceptance.

Example: On Tripadvisor, millions rely on user reviews and rankings to select hotels or restaurants. Even with brand advertising, consumers often default to peer opinions for final judgments.

7.3.2 User-Generated Content (UGC)

User-generated content refers to photos, videos, stories, or reviews created by a brand's audience, rather than by the brand itself. Because UGC stems from real users, it resonates more strongly with skeptics who prefer unbiased opinions.

Methods for gathering UGC

To foster a steady flow of UGC, brands can make it fun and easy for customers to participate. They must invite users to share personal stories, photos, or experiences linked to the brand's main themes. By offering clear instructions, such as hashtags or prompts, and responding promptly to submissions, they can enable participants to feel recognized.

Brands can show appreciation by reposting outstanding content or providing small incentives like shout-outs, feature spots, or exclusive discounts. They should also regularly remind the community that their creativity and feedback matter, and be transparent about how the brand might use these contributions.

1. **Hashtag campaigns**

   Encouraging users to post content (photos, short videos) under a unified hashtag fosters community. For instance, a sports brand might use #MyDailyRun to gather fitness journeys from everyday runners.

2. **Contests and challenges**

   Offering small prizes or recognition for the best user-submitted designs, recipes, or creative brand uses can spur high engagement.

3. Community spotlights

Featuring outstanding user contributions on official brand platforms helps to appreciate fans for their loyalty and entices others to participate.

7.3.3 Moderation and ethics

User-driven platforms offer considerable benefits, yet they also present notable challenges. On one hand, honest user contributions establish trust and strengthen credibility. On the other hand, negative, misleading, or defamatory content can undermine the community if left unchecked or censored too aggressively.

To strike a balance, businesses should create clear, transparent brand guidelines that specify acceptable behavior and content. Removing hateful or spam-filled posts protects the community's well-being, while allowing legitimate criticism can reveal growth opportunities and demonstrate respect for open dialogue.

Ownership and permission policies are just as vital. Brands should ask for explicit consent or clarify terms of use before reposting user-generated images, artwork, or written content. This not only honors the creator's rights but also upholds ethical standards that resonate with consumers. Consistent enforcement of these guidelines helps maintain a supportive atmosphere. It preserves the sense of authenticity that user-driven platforms can provide.

POINT TO REMEMBER

Reposting user photos or stories can delight fans, but only if it respects intellectual property rights. Always clarify terms or ask for direct permission. When used ethically, spotlighting UGC fosters deeper brand loyalty as contributors see their creative expressions recognized.

Throughout this chapter, we examined how brand communications and marketing create a cohesive public image. From unified messaging across channels to encouraging user-generated content, each approach is most effective when it aligns with the brand's core identity. By integrating social proof, respecting ethical standards in moderation, and maintaining transparency in every interaction, managers can strengthen overall brand equity. Chapter 8 will expand on managing brand performance, revealing how data-driven insights can guide continued growth and adaptation in a competitive marketplace.

Chapter Summary

- Unified communication across multiple platforms prevents confusion and reinforces a single, coherent brand identity.

- Cross-channel consistency involves aligning visuals, tone, and themes. This helps users have the same brand impression whether online, in print, or in person.

- Brand equity stems from factors like brand awareness, perceived quality, associations, and loyalty. All of these factors contribute to intangible market value.

- Strategic repetition—through brand assets such as logos, slogans, and mascots—enhances recognition and helps messages stick.

- Partnerships, sponsorships, and frequent yet consistent exposure expand brand familiarity faster than isolated efforts.

- Protecting brand equity requires mindful expansions or updates that don't conflict with core values. A strong brand can leverage loyalty to branch into new arenas.

- Social proof, including reviews, influencer endorsements, and peer ratings, significantly influences purchase decisions, often more than direct brand statements.

- User-generated content adds authenticity. Audiences trust real consumer stories and experiences over polished corporate ads.

- Fostering UGC through hashtag campaigns or contests builds active communities. However, it demands transparent moderation to address spam or inappropriate content.

- Balancing global brand identity with local cultural nuances ensures relevance and acceptance in diverse regions without diluting brand fundamentals.

- Consistent efforts to listen, respond, and improve brand communications maintain audience trust, especially during crises or controversies.

- Combining an omnichannel approach with carefully curated brand messages drives synergy. It enables each marketing channel to reinforce the others.

- Ethical guidelines in community management, such as respecting intellectual property and avoiding censorship of constructive criticism, preserve trust and engagement.

- Long-term success hinges on adapting strategies to emerging trends while retaining the brand's distinctive voice, values, and visual hallmarks.

Quiz

1. **Which statement best defines cross-channel consistency?**

    a. Presenting different brand messages on each platform to test creative variety

    b. Maintaining uniform brand voice and appearance across all touchpoints

    c. Restricting brand presence to a single channel at a time

    d. Changing color palettes monthly to keep audiences guessing

2. **How can organizations overcome siloed communications among different teams?**

    a. By assigning contradictory brand guidelines to each department

    b. By eliminating internal memos or brand style guides

    c. Through collaboration, shared brand guidelines, and integrated campaign planning

    d. By relying on freelancers for each marketing channel

3. **Why might a brand adapt its messaging locally in international markets?**

    a. To confuse consumers about brand identity

    b. Because brand visuals are irrelevant in new locations

    c. To address cultural nuances while retaining the brand's central values

    d. To lower production costs by ignoring a global brand identity

4. **What is one benefit of using traditional media like print or radio alongside digital marketing?**

   a. It ensures the brand never appears on social platforms.

   b. It prevents data collection from consumer interactions.

   c. It broadens reach and offers multiple reinforcing brand impressions.

   d. It complicates brand messaging to appear more "authentic."

5. **Which element is not typically part of brand equity's core components?**

   a. Brand awareness

   b. Perceived quality

   c. Public domain images unrelated to the brand

   d. Emotional brand associations

6. **Perceived quality refers to:**

   a. The exact manufacturing cost of the brand's flagship product

   b. How consumers view the brand's overall reliability, desirability, or prestige

   c. Legal certifications required for product safety

   d. A fixed measure unaffected by consumer reviews

7. **In building brand recognition, "distinctive brand assets" might include:**

   a. A standard 12-digit product barcode

   b. Memorable jingles, unique color schemes, or iconic logos

   c. Randomized brand slogans used once on social media

   d. Unbranded packaging to save costs

8. **Which of the following is a potential risk of brand overextension?**

   a. Enhancing consumer confidence in all product categories

   b. Strengthening the original brand by providing diverse product lines

   c. Diluting brand meaning if new offerings conflict with established brand identity

   d. Guaranteeing automatic success in foreign markets

9. **A brand's intangible "license to charge a premium" is tied to:**

   a. Government regulation on luxury goods

   b. Strong brand equity that justifies higher prices

   c. The absence of direct competitors in the market

   d. Strict adherence to minimal marketing budgets

10. **How might brand managers gauge brand equity quantitatively?**

    a. Through random guesses or speculation about brand performance

    b. By analyzing consumer surveys, price premiums, market share, and financial valuation

    c. By relying on anecdotal evidence from internal staff

    d. By ignoring brand associations or loyalty metrics

Answers

1 – b	2 – c	3 – c	4 – c	5 – c
6 – b	7 – b	8 – c	9 – b	10 – b

CHAPTER 8

Managing Brand Performance

Key Learning Objectives

- Explain the importance of measuring brand performance across multiple dimensions, including awareness, loyalty, and equity.
- Identify and apply key performance metrics to assess the health and trajectory of a brand.
- Develop strategies to adapt brand approaches based on data-driven insights.
- Examine methods to remain relevant in dynamic markets influenced by technology, competition, and cultural shifts.
- Plan for long-term brand success by integrating forward-looking strategies, continuous innovation, and stakeholder value creation.
- Implement practical guidelines that align performance measurement with the brand's strategic goals and evolving customer expectations.

Everything we have covered so far, from positioning and personality to experience design and communication, only earns its keep if it improves results. Brand performance measurement knits these strands together, showing in clear numbers whether a brand is gaining ground or drifting off course. Awareness, loyalty, and equity convert big ideas into evidence, exposing strengths, gaps, and the next levers to pull.

In this final chapter, we will learn to translate these measures into action. First, we will learn to set firm benchmarks so brand health is never left to guesswork. Then, we'll discuss how to collect and read data fast enough to adjust courses in real-time. Finally, we outline ways to keep a brand moving as technology, culture, and competitors shift. Treat this chapter as the operating manual that ties every concept in the book together and keeps the brand strong long after launch.

8.1 Key Metrics: Awareness, Loyalty, Equity

Performance data only matters if it maps cleanly onto the journey a consumer takes with the brand. Across industries, three checkpoints keep surfacing in academic work and in the operating dashboards of high-growth brands:

1. **Awareness:** Do people recall us at the moment of need?
2. **Loyalty:** Do they come back, and do they defend us in conversation?
3. **Equity:** Can our name command a premium or forgive the occasional misstep?

These layers sit on top of one another like steps; weaken the lower tread and the higher one soon sags. Figure 8.1 summarizes this relationship.

Figure 8.1 | The A-L-E Ladder of Brand Health

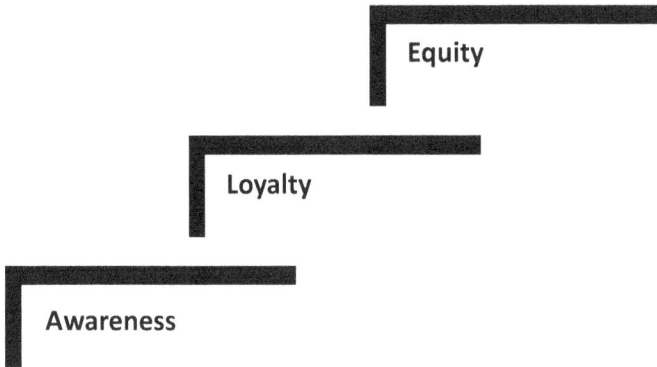

Equity

Loyalty

Awareness

8.1.1 Awareness metrics

Awareness metrics show how often people notice or recall your brand. When customers never see or recognize you, it is almost impossible to build a deeper connection. By measuring awareness, you learn whether your brand has entered the minds of potential buyers and whether they can recall it at key moments.

1. **Aided and unaided recall**

    Aided recall tests if people recognize your brand when given a direct cue, such as a logo, slogan, or product category. Unaided recall checks whether they can bring up your brand name on their own, without any help (Keller, 2016).

A shopper may recognize a logo when shown (aided), yet fail to name the brand when standing in front of the shelf (unaided). A wide gap between aided and unaided recall often means people only recognize you with a hint. This indicates that the brand is not "top-of-mind" in real-life scenarios.

Example: A 2022 YouGov RealTime survey of Indonesian consumers found that 88% recalled Ramadan commercials from fruit-syrup brand Marjan when prompted (aided), yet only 60% named Marjan unaided as the first brand that came to mind for Ramadan ads (YouGov, 2022). This 28-point gap shows how catchy ads can outperform actual brand recall.

2. **Share of Voice (SOV) and Share of Search (SOS)**

   These metrics measure how often your brand is mentioned or searched for compared to others in your market. A high share of voice or search suggests you are leading the conversation, but if your competitors' numbers climb faster, it may be time to revise your brand messaging or marketing channels (Nielsen, 2009), (Binet & Les, 2020).

   Example: A brand might own 25% of all media mentions in its category (high SOV), yet attract only 10% of search-engine queries for that category (low SOS). The gap tells managers that people hear the message but don't feel moved to look for the brand. This signals that the creative or call-to-action needs work.

3. Social media reach and impressions

Reach shows how many individual people see your content, while impressions count how many total times your content is shown (including repeats to the same person).

> **TIP** High reach or impressions are good, but you should also track the interactions that show genuine interest. Numbers that look big may not mean real engagement or brand loyalty.

Table 8.1 Key awareness metrics

Metric	Primary question	Collection methods and frequency examples
Unaided recall	"Do buyers name us first?"	Ask 500+ consumers to name the first brand they think of in your category. Run once per quarter.
Aided recall	"Do buyers recognize our cue?"	Show your logo or package and record the percentage of people who recognized it. Do this in the same quarterly survey.
Share of Voice	"How loud are we vs. rivals?"	Add up monthly ad spend and media mentions for all brands; calculate your share. Review each month.
Share of Search	"Who wins with intent traffic?"	Download brand-query data from tools such as Google Trends, and divide by total category searches. Check monthly.
Reach and Impressions	"How far do we broadcast?"	Pull reach (unique viewers) and impressions (total views) from social-platform dashboards every week.

Source: (Adapted from Keller 2016; Nielsen 2009; Binet & Les 2020.)

Interpreting awareness metrics

When interpreting awareness metrics, brand managers should be on the lookout for patterns. Make sure to ask: Is awareness improving every month or quarter, or is it stalled? Compare your awareness levels to close competitors so you know whether you are improving in a meaningful way or just keeping pace.

> **TIP** Note which platforms or advertising channels generate the most growth, so you can invest more in what works best.

8.1.2 Loyalty metrics

Once people know your brand, the next question is whether they come back for more. Loyalty metrics tell you if customers trust your offerings enough to make repeated purchases and recommend you to their friends. This trust can be invaluable because loyal buyers usually spend more over time and encourage others to try your brand.

Common loyalty metrics include:

1. Repeat Purchase Rate (RPR)
2. Customer Lifetime Value (CLV)
3. Net Promoter Score (NPS)
4. Engagement and Advocacy Rate

1. Repeat Purchase Rate (RPR)

The RPR measures the percentage of customers who make another purchase within a certain period. Seeing a steady climb in RPR often means a product or service lives up to expectations. From this, brand managers can infer whether customers are making their brand a habit.

RPR = *Number of buyers with at least two purchases in a defined time period/ Total number of buyers in that defined time period*

Example: 1,200 unique customers placed at least one order in Q1. 360 of them returned to buy again before the quarter ended. **RPR is 360/ 1200 = 30%.** This shows that roughly one in three buyers became repeat purchasers within the same 90-day window.

2. **Customer Lifetime Value (CLV)**

    CLV estimates the total amount of money a single customer might spend on your brand throughout the entire relationship. A high CLV can justify investments in loyalty programs or premium perks. If a brand manager knows a customer will likely spend a certain amount over the years, they can plan retention strategies more effectively.

    CLV = *Average basket size (amount spent per order)* × *Average number of orders per year* × *Typical retention years.*

    Example: If the average shopper spends $40 per order, buys 3 times a year, and stays for 4 years, their **CLV = $40 × 3 × 4 = $480.**

    Brand managers should re-evaluate at least twice a year to reflect new prices and identify buying habits, or churn.

3. **Net Promoter Score (NPS)**

    Recall from Chapter 7 that the NPS measures whether customers would recommend you to someone else. It is based on a 0-10 scale, with 9-10 being "Promoters," 7-8 being "Passives," and 0-6 being "Detractors." A strong NPS usually means customers are satisfied. It also means they are eager to help spread the word. A low NPS may indicate frustration or unmet expectations.

$$\textbf{NPS} = \text{Percentage of Promoters - Percentage of Detractors}$$

Example: A brand manager receives 100 survey responses. 55 are Promoters (9-10) and 20 are Detractors (0-6). The **NPS = 55% – 20% = +35.** In this case, the brand has more advocates than critics. However, it still sits below the +50 "excellent" threshold, indicating room for improvement.

To capture NPS effectively, brand managers should ask the recommendation question in a post-purchase email or text within 7 days of the customer receiving the product or service.

4. Engagement and advocacy rate

This looks at how often people mention, review, or share your brand voluntarily, for example, through social media posts or word-of-mouth. Advocacy suggests a deeper form of loyalty. Measure by counting tagged user posts and positive reviews in a given month. Then, weigh each by follower reach or star rating. Finally, divide by the total volume of brand mentions to spot shifts in sentiment.

Example: A brand logs 400 social mentions in a month. 100 are positive, tagged recommendations. The advocacy rate is **100 ÷ 400 = 25%.** This indicates that one in four conversations is an unpaid endorsement, signalling solid advocacy.

POINT TO REMEMBER

Brand managers need to watch how loyalty changes over time. If repeat purchases dip or if negative word-of-mouth rises, it may be a sign of unmet needs or strong competition.

DISCUSSION

Pretend you are a brand manager and your NPS has risen for three straight quarters, yet the repeat-purchase rate is flat. List two possible reasons for this mismatch and describe what data you would check next.

8.1.3 Equity metrics

Even if people are aware of your brand and buy from it, long-term strength often lies in brand equity.

Brand equity: The added value that a brand name and reputation bring to what would otherwise be a generic product or service (Keller, 2016).

Higher brand equity allows for higher prices, more loyalty, and greater resilience in tough markets. When buyers prefer a brand, chances are the equity is strong. This is true even if competitors offer similar products at lower prices. Brand managers usually assess equity through the following four ways outlined in Table 8.2:

1. Brand perception surveys
2. Price premium
3. Financial brand valuation
4. Emotional equity indicators

Table 8.2	Measuring brand equity	

Method	What it measures	Why it matters
Brand perception surveys	Customer ratings of quality, authenticity, relevance vs. key rivals	Falling scores signal the need to fine-tune positioning before revenue slips
Price premium	Difference between your average selling price and a store-brand or budget option	A stable or rising gap shows buyers are willing to pay for the name
Financial brand valuation	Dollar value of the brand asset.	Quantifies brand strength for investors, mergers and acquisitions, or licensing decisions
Emotional equity indicators	Trust, admiration, and "brand love" from sentiment analysis	Strong emotion lowers price sensitivity, boosts word-of-mouth, and acts as a shock absorber when negative news hits

Source: (Adapted from Keller, 2016 & Aaker, 1996).

Brand managers should look for alignment in these measures. A brand with a high price premium but low emotional scores is living on borrowed time. In contrast, a brand with high love but no premium may have room to raise its margin.

Recall from Chapter 4 that a **perceptual map** is a visual positioning tool that shows how customers view your brand compared to competitors based on key attributes. Perceptual maps can be a valuable tool for brand managers when measuring brand equity.

Figure 8.2 presents a perceptual map that plots eight competing brands along two common equity signals: **perceived quality** (horizontal axis) and **selling-price index** (vertical axis). In this example, the brand manager has gathered feedback from customers regarding the perceived quality of each competing brand on a seven-point scale, where 1 indicates very low perceived quality and 7 indicates very high perceived quality. A price index expresses a brand's average shelf price as a percentage of a chosen reference (often the store-brand or category average, set at 100). In Figure 8.2, the store brand anchors the scale at 100. A brand indexed at 120 sells for roughly 20 percent more than the store brand, while one at 80 sells for about 20 percent less.

Figure 8.2 Perceived Quality vs. Price Perceptual Map

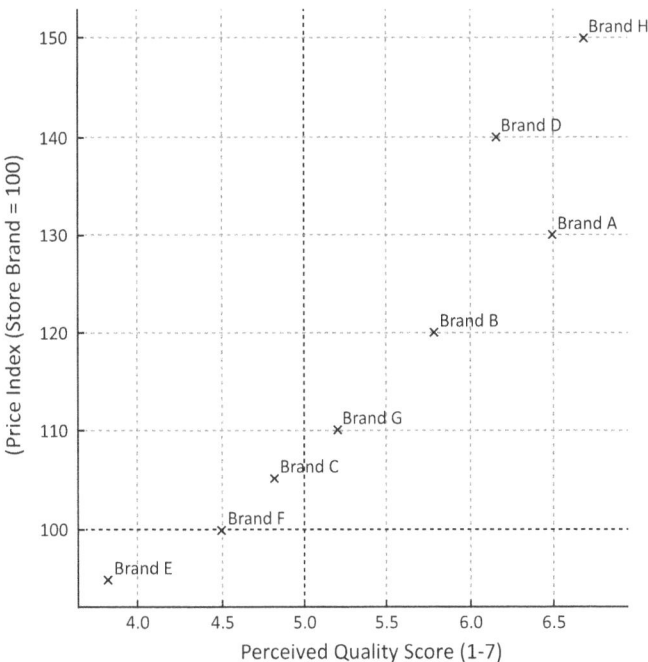

In this example, brands in the upper-right quadrant (high quality and high premium) have the strongest equity positions. Customers rate these brands as superior and are generally happy to pay a little extra for them. Brands clustered in the lower-left indicate the opposite, low-quality perception and little or no price power. By tracking movement on this map each quarter, brand managers see whether changes in product experience, messaging, or pricing strategy are measurably strengthening (or diminishing) the brand's equity over time.

> **POINT TO REMEMBER**
>
> Trust and admiration usually fade before price-premium shrinks. Brand managers should treat a dip in emotional equity as an early warning for future margin pressure.

8.2 Measuring Performance and Adapting Strategy

Numbers become valuable only when they turn into timely decisions. In this section, we'll identify the main sources of brand data. Then, we'll learn to combine those streams into a single dashboard. Finally, we will understand how to respond when any metric signals a problem.

8.2.1 Data collection and analysis frameworks

A reliable brand dashboard starts with knowing where the facts live and how each source adds a different angle on performance. Five data sources shown in Figure 8.3 cover the essentials, ranging from granular, person-level behavior to broad revenue totals. These sources, from the top down, include sales and revenue, which reflect broad revenue totals. These are followed by surveys, web, and social media platforms, which give a broad view of customer behavior. At the bottom of the pyramid are Customer-Relationship-Management (CRM) systems, which provide the personal-level customer behavior insights.

Figure 8.3 Data-Source Pyramid

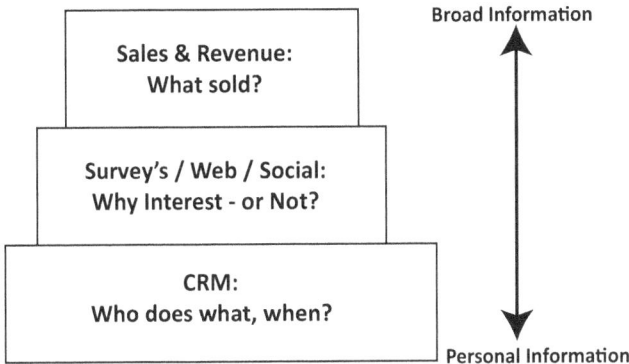

1. **CRM systems**

   A CRM system records every order, return, email click, and support ticket. Because each entry ties to a customer ID, it shows patterns that no survey can catch, such as first-90-day churn, purchase frequency, and cross-sell success. For instance, brand managers should run a "new-buyer churn" report monthly. A spike tells you to inspect onboarding or product quality.

2. **Surveys and qualitative research**

   Surveys assign numbers to perceived quality, authenticity, and relevance. Interviews and focus groups uncover motives. A quarterly brand tracker paired with one annual deep-dive group ensures both breadth and depth.

A brand tracker is a recurring survey (usually run every quarter) that asks the same core questions each time. Because the questions stay constant, you can spot real movement rather than random survey noise. Think of it as a "health-check report card" for the brand: every three months, you take the same readings and plot the trend line. If quality perception drops two waves in a row while a competitor rises, you know where to focus the next quarter's resources.

A basic brand tracker covers:

- **Salience:** unaided and aided recall
- **Perception:** quality, authenticity, relevance scores
- **Intention:** customer likelihood to try, repurchase, or recommend
- **Competitive set:** using the same metrics as your key rivals

Launch the tracker within two weeks of a major campaign. Fresh memory yields clearer results than a month-old impression.

3. Digital analytics

Web and app analytics trace where curiosity dies (e.g., 70% exit on the shipping page) or where features stick. Review where drop-offs occur once a week. Pages losing the most traffic need copy, offer, or load-speed fixes.

CRM shows who stays; digital analytics show where others leave. Check both before rewriting ads or discounting products.

4. Social listening

Listening tools scan public posts for volume and sentiment, offering a real-time radar on buzz or issues.

Example: A snack brand spotted Reddit chatter about "stale chips" hours after a factory glitch. A same-day apology plus vouchers contained the story, and NPS never dipped.

5. Sales and revenue data

Units, price, and margin confirm whether upstream improvements translate into purchases. Align weekly sales with campaign dates; if awareness jumps but revenue stalls, re-examine the offer, price, or distribution rather than adding more media.

DISCUSSION

Consider a scenario where social listening shows a spike in negative comments, yet CRM repeat-purchase is steady. Name two possible reasons for the mismatch and cite one extra data source you'd pull to verify your hunch.

8.2.2 Creating a brand performance dashboard

A brand dashboard is a single online page that can even be as simple as a shared spreadsheet. The dashboard pulls key numbers from different systems and places them side-by-side. With one glance, a brand manager should be able to answer three questions:

1.   Are people noticing us? (visibility)
2.   Are they acting? (engagement and sales)
3.   Are we still earning our premium? (loyalty and equity)

The first question a brand manager should ask when building their performance dashboard is, "Where should my numbers come from?" Almost every business, even a small venture or side hustle, can collect at least one metric from each of these four places:

1.   **Website or app analytics:** Free tools such as Google Analytics list visits, bounce rate, and most-viewed pages.
2.   **Social-platform insights:** Instagram, TikTok, and X all offer a built-in tab that counts views, saves, and shares.
3.   **Sales or Point of Sale (POS) systems:** An e-commerce backend (Shopify or WooCommerce, for example) or a café's register/till records units sold, average tickets, and refunds.
4.   **Quick surveys:** A three-question Google Form emailed after purchase can capture customer satisfaction and willingness to recommend.

Example: An independent coffee roaster pulls four basic measures to add to its dashboard:

1. "Visits to our Beans page" from website analytics. This measures online interest.

2. Post-saves for new-blend photos from Instagram Insights. This measures creative appeal.

3. Cups sold per day from the café till. This measures purchases.

4. NPS score from a short follow-up survey to measure customer satisfaction.

TIP Start with one metric per source. Add new metrics only when a clear business question appears; otherwise, the screen becomes noise.

Plotted together, these four readings already tell the owner whether marketing sparks interest, the café converts that interest, and customers leave happy.

DISCUSSION
Imagine you manage a small skincare brand that just launched a viral TikTok video. Website traffic has doubled, but the number of completed checkouts and your average order value are unchanged. You can add only one new dial to your dashboard this month. Which metric would you choose, and from which data source, to understand what's preventing sales, and why?

8.2.3 Interpreting results and taking action

A dashboard is only useful when its metrics lead to clear decisions. The easiest way to read any metric is to run it through three questions:

1. **Level:** Is the number where you expected it to be?
2. **Trend:** Has it been moving in the same direction long enough to matter?
3. **Relationship:** Does a related metric confirm or contradict what you are seeing?

This simple Level-Trend-Relationship (LTR) scan turns raw numbers into practical insight (Farris et al., 2010). When you apply LTR to each KPI on the dashboard you built in Section 8.2.2 above, the screen stops being a set of isolated metrics and becomes a diagnostic tool.

Table 8.3 summarizes how to use each lens and offers beginner-friendly rules of thumb.

Table 8.3   **The LTR Scan at a glance**

Lens	Ask yourself	Practical guideline
Level	Is the metric on or off target?	Within 5 percent of the goal: stay the course. More than 5 percent off: flag for review.
Trend	Is the change temporary or persistent?	One-period (a blip): make note of it. Two periods: investigate. Three periods: prepare an action plan.
Relationship	Do paired metrics tell the same story?	Rising awareness should pair with rising clicks; if not, check messages or call to action.

Source: (Adapted from Farris et al., 2010)

Use the thresholds in Table 8.3 as a starting point. If a brand operates in a category with tighter margins (e.g., groceries), brand managers may act on smaller deviations. Conversely, brands in slower-moving markets (e.g., B2B software) might wait for larger swings.

Taking action

Once the LTR scan flags a problem, you need a way to fix it without risking the whole brand. The most practical method is a micro-experiment loop. Think of it as a miniature scientific method for marketers, based on the following pillars:

- **Focus:** change one element at a time, so you know what caused any shift.

- **Speed:** keep the test short (two to four weeks) so results inform the next cycle quickly.

- **Evidence:** measure one outcome that links directly to the drift you saw on the dashboard.

The Five-Step Micro-Experiment Loop

It's a small, time-boxed test, often running for two to four weeks, that changes one thing and measures one outcome. Each pass through the loop answers a single question: "Will this level move the stuck metric?" and the answer guides the next action. Let's look at the five steps below:

Table 8.4 | **The Five-Step Micro-Experiment Loop**

Step	Ask	Example
1. Identify the drift	What changed?	The checkout completion rate fell three percentage points in April.
2. Form a hypothesis	Why did it happen?	Visitors abandon when unexpected shipping fees appear late in the funnel.
3. Choose a lever	What single change will we test?	Show shipping cost on the product page for 50% of visitors (A/B split).

Step	Ask	Example
4. Run the test	How long and what will we measure?	Two-week A/B test; success target = regain two points of checkout completion.
5. Lock in or rollback	Keep the change or revert?	If the test group meets the target, roll out to 100% of traffic; if not, revert and test the next hypothesis (e.g., payment options).

Source: (Adapted from Lafley et. al, 2015)

Repeating this loop each month builds a culture of evidence-based tweaks instead of opinion-based redesigns.

FUN FACT

Booking.com runs over 25,000 micro-experiments each year. This equates to more than 60 at any given moment. Fewer than one in ten tests delivers a measurable lift on its own, but the small wins compound into hundreds of millions of euros in extra bookings (Harvard Business Review, 2020).

8.3 Staying Relevant in Changing Markets

You now have the knowledge pertaining to reading dashboards and running small experiments to keep day-to-day performance on track. While those skills are vital, it's important to remember that markets change—sometimes quietly, sometimes overnight. A brand that fails to see a shift early can lose hard-won equity rapidly.

In this section, you will learn how to look outward. Technologies evolve, consumer values swing, new rivals appear, and regulations tighten or loosen. An effective business can watch the wider environment, spot changes early, and adjust while still preserving the qualities that customers already love.

8.3.1 Scanning the environment

A brand does not operate in a vacuum; external forces can lift it or squeeze it, no matter how well the internal dashboard looks. Systematic environmental scanning helps brands see those forces early enough to react with product tweaks, new messages, or fresh distribution plans. Three lenses are most common:

1. **PESTEL analysis:** A wide-angle scan of Political, Economic, Social, Technological, Environmental, and Legal factors.
2. **Competitive-landscape mapping:** a close-up view of what rivals, substitutes, and disruptors are doing.
3. **Cultural and social-trend tracking:** a feel for the mood swings that make messages land or miss.

Used together, these tools keep the brand alert without losing focus on its core promise.

1. PESTEL Analysis

PESTEL is a six-factor checklist (Fig. 8.4) used in strategy work (Johnson, Scholes & Whittington 2005). Each external factor can impact a brand's positioning, portfolio, or purpose.

| Figure 8.4 | PESTEL Analysis |

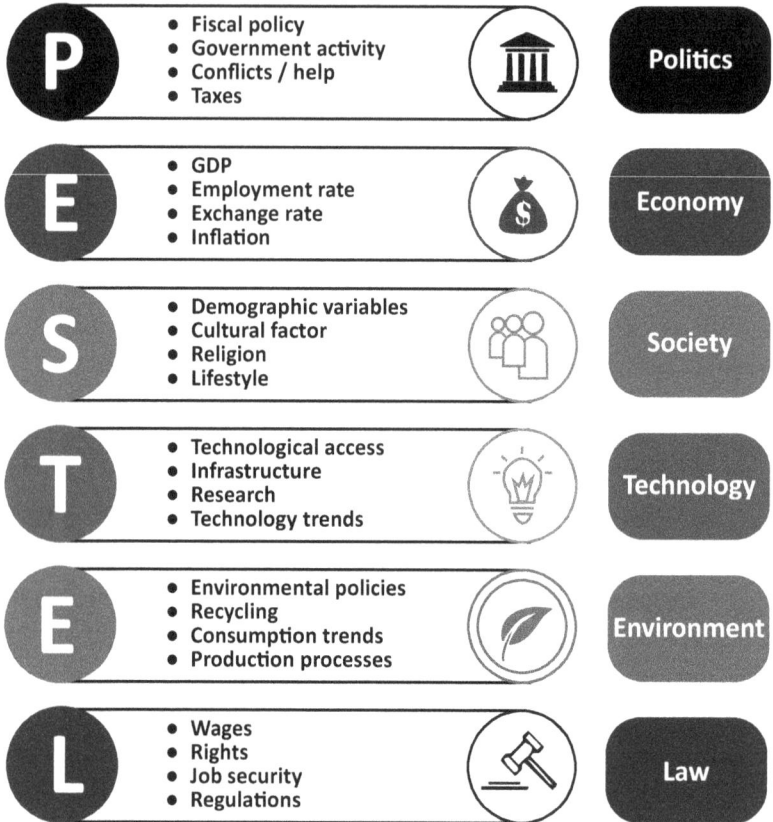

P	• Fiscal policy • Government activity • Conflicts / help • Taxes	Politics
E	• GDP • Employment rate • Exchange rate • Inflation	Economy
S	• Demographic variables • Cultural factor • Religion • Lifestyle	Society
T	• Technological access • Infrastructure • Research • Technology trends	Technology
E	• Environmental policies • Recycling • Consumption trends • Production processes	Environment
L	• Wages • Rights • Job security • Regulations	Law

(Management & Strategy Institute, 2024)

Source: (Management & Strategy Institute, 2024)

Table 8.5 outlines various external scenarios that may impact the strategy of a brand.

Table 8.5 PESTEL Analysis

Factor	Brand impact	Brand action
Political	Will a new policy collide with our stated purpose?	A sports-drink brand that champions "everyday athletes" publicly backs community-field funding to align with a government wellness push.
Economic	Do income shifts threaten our price tier?	A premium skincare label launches a "starter" sub-brand to keep aspirational shoppers during a recession.
Social	Are emerging values at odds with our tone?	A decades-old razor brand drops macho taglines and reframes its promise around "skin confidence for all genders."
Technological	Could new technology redefine brand experience?	A heritage furniture brand creates an AR app so customers can place pieces in their living rooms, updating its craftsmanship story for a digital era.
Legal	Will regulation alter how we express benefits?	A supplement brand rewrites pack copy to emphasize "supports" rather than "cures," protecting trust as health-claim rules tighten.
Environmental	Do eco-pressures demand a visible stance?	A bottled-water brand pivots to aluminum cans and re-launches under the narrative "Pure water, zero plastic," refreshing its identity around sustainability.

2. Competitive landscape

Knowing who else is trying to win your customer's attention tells you where to defend, where to differentiate, and where unmet needs still exist. Brand managers scan three layers of competition, outlined in Table 8.6, to answer these questions.

Table 8.6 **Layers of competition**

Layer	Who's in it	What to study
Direct rivals	Those who sell almost the same product or service	Pricing, feature set, tone of voice: are you distinct enough?
Indirect substitutes	Those who solve the same problem in a different way	Benefit promise and occasion of use: could they steal your usage moments?
Disruptive entrants	Those who use new technology or a new model to change the rules	Speed of adoption, funding strength, and whether their story reframes the category

When evaluating the competitive landscape, brand managers and businesses should be on the lookout for:

- **Positioning overlap:** Are two brands claiming the same core benefit?

- **Price-for-value gaps:** Is anyone offering more for the same price—or the same for less?

- **Narrative whitespace:** Which customer needs or occasions are not yet spoken for?

- **Signature assets:** Logos, colors, and experiences that competitors "own" first.

> **POINT TO REMEMBER** A true competitor is any solution the customer might choose *instead* of you. Sometimes that's a different brand, but it could also be a substitute, or when the customer simply takes no action.

3. Cultural and social trends

Cultural shifts such as gender roles, work patterns, and sustainability concerns shape what messaging feels authentic. Social listening, consumer-trend reports, and even TikTok hashtags help brand teams sense these undercurrents.

Example: The quiet luxury trend that emerged in 2023 pushed several fashion labels to mute visible logos and emphasize fabric provenance. This aligned better with consumers' new preference for known quality over loud status.

8.3.2 Customer-centric innovation

While environmental scanning tells you what is changing, customer-centric innovation decides how your brand will answer. Customer-centric innovation refers to the practice of prioritizing enhancements that solve a clear customer problem or unlock a desired outcome, even when the change is not a brand-new product (Christensen, 2016).

| Figure 8.5 | Customer-centric innovation |

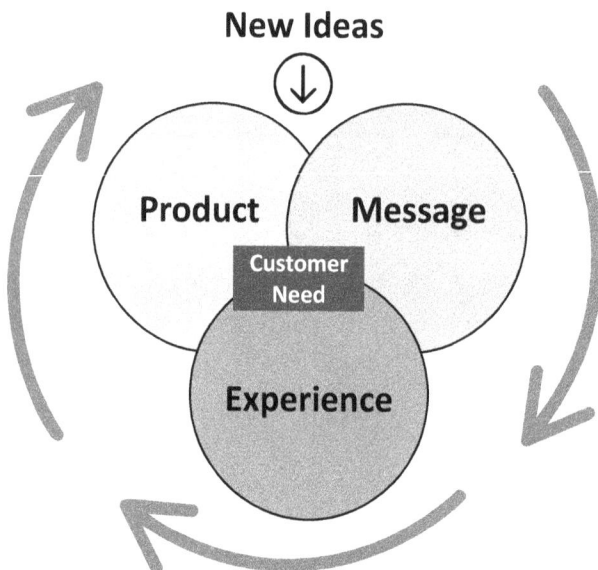

This means shaping any new idea, whether it be a product, message, service, or channel-related aspect, around a validated customer need rather than around internal excitement over a technology. When innovation stays anchored to real pain points, it deepens relevance instead of adding random features.

Below are the three innovation paths that brand teams pursue most often. Each starts with the same question: "What is the next barrier or aspiration for our customer?"

Table 8.7 Customer-centric innovation paths

Path	Brand-focused aim	Example
Product innovation	Keep the offer fresh while staying true to the brand promise	A premium yogurt brand adds a "zero-sugar kids pouch" to satisfy health-conscious parents without diluting its gourmet positioning.
Message and marketing innovation	Refresh how the brand story reaches people.	A classic shoemaker joins TikTok's #Restitch trend, showing 30-second repair hacks to underline durability, a core equity it already owns.
Experience and channel innovation	Remove friction or add delight wherever the brand is met.	A heritage watch label introduces virtual try-on in its app, letting shoppers angle the dial on their own wrist before stepping into a boutique.

Source: (Adapted from Christensen 2016, Kotler & Keller 2016)

8.3.3 Repositioning and rebranding

Scanning the environment tells you *what* is shifting; customer-centric innovation shows *how* to refresh offerings and experiences. Occasionally, though, market signals point to something bigger. When the position the brand occupies in people's minds or even the brand's visible identity no longer fits the world around it, that is when managers face two crucial tools, repositioning and rebranding:

> **TIP** Keep a running idea backlog fed by reviews, support calls, and social comments. Tag each suggestion P (Product), M (Message), or E (Experience). Review the list monthly and promote one item per category into small-scale testing.

1. **Repositioning:** Adjusting *who* the brand is for or *which benefit* it promises while keeping most visual assets intact.

Example: Pepsi's 1984 "New Generation" campaign shifted category perceptions. Before this repositioning effort, Pepsi and Coca-Cola clustered near the center on a positioning map (Fig. 8.6).

Pepsi was seen as mildly youthful but not strongly differentiated. Coca-Cola (Coke) held a slight heritage advantage without being viewed as old. By explicitly claiming the *young/ modern* quadrant and pairing it with contemporary music-video imagery, Pepsi vaulted up and right on the map, owning the youthful-modern position. Because perceptual space is zero-sum, that same messaging implicitly nudged Coke down and left toward dated/ old, even though Coca-Cola changed nothing about its product.

Figure 8.6 **Pepsi brand repositioning**

Impact of Pepsi's "New Generation" Campaign

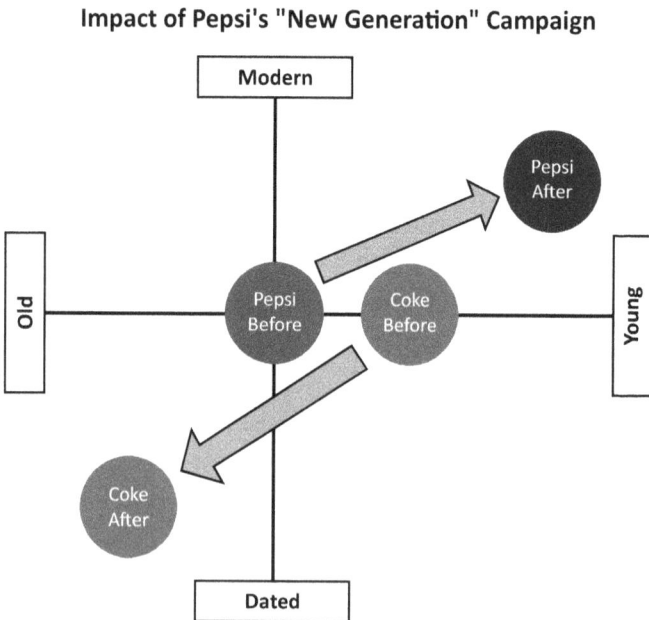

Source: (Fripp, 2023)

2. **Rebranding:** Changing name, logo, colors, or tone because the old signals block growth or cause confusion.

Example: In 2018, after 68 years under the "Donuts" banner, Dunkin' Donuts officially became simply Dunkin'. They rolled out a cleaner wordmark and a brighter, more modern color palette to underscore its growing emphasis on coffee and other beverages (Dunkin', 2018). By removing the narrow "Donuts" label, the company clarified its broader menu offerings, reduced consumer confusion, and positioned itself for future growth beyond its traditional pastry roots. The visual identity remained familiar by maintaining the playful pink and orange color scheme and bold sans-serif font, thus preserving brand recognition while signaling evolution. This approach exemplifies how brands can modernize while retaining key visual elements for continuity.

Repositioning can extend a brand's life for a decade, whereas a full rebrand is closer to "strategic surgery" and should be rare (Aaker, 1996).

DISCUSSION

Your sports-drink brand owns the promise "hydrates faster." New science shows every brand in the aisle now offers similar hydration speed, but your bright-blue bottle is still well recognized. Would you recommend repositioning or full rebranding? Explain which assets you would keep, change, or drop, and why.

8.3.4 Agility in brand management

Repositioning and rebranding are heavyweight moves that happen only occasionally. Agility is what keeps a brand lively in the weeks and months between those big swings.

Brand agility: The ability to **sense** change early, **decide** quickly, **act** in small increments, and **learn** just as fast (McKinsey, 2019). Think of it as a rolling loop that never stops.

| Figure 8.7 | The Brand Agility Loop |

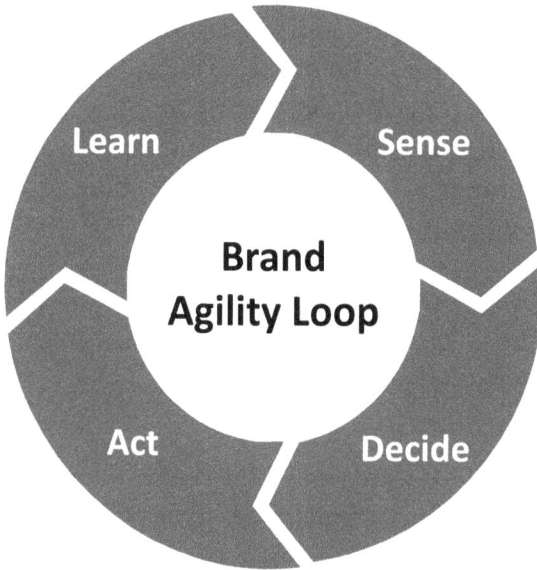

Small daily check-ins on social chatter, brief weekly tweaks to copy, offer, or service flow, and a quick review every fortnight keep that loop spinning in real-time.

By stringing together many such micro-adjustments, a brand stays relevant without diluting the core promise that larger repositioning efforts protect. This everyday agility forms the bridge between the environmental scanning we have just learned and the multi-year roadmap we turn to in the next section.

8.4 Planning for Long-Term Brand Success

The previous chapters in this book have trained you to define, measure, and tune a brand in real-time. This closing section steps back and asks a larger, long-term question: How do you keep the brand healthy for the next five-plus years?

The answer lies in four practices: road mapping, cultural embedding, resourcing innovation, and risk preparedness. These practices stitch the short-term tactics you've learned together into a lasting advantage.

8.4.1 Build a multi-horizon roadmap

Sustaining relevance means working on today, tomorrow, and the day after, all at once. The Three-Horizon Framework (Baghai, Coley, & White, 1999) divides a brand's plans into parallel time bands.

Table 8.8	Three-Horizon Framework		

Horizon	Typical span	Guiding question	Sample activities
H1 – Sustain	0-12 months	"How do we meet this year's targets?"	Campaign calendar, quarterly KPI reviews
H2 – Expand	Years 1-3	"Where will we grow next?"	New segments, line extensions, channel upgrades
H3 – Reinvent	Years 3-5+	"What could redefine us?"	Breakthrough products, new purpose initiatives

Source: (Adapted from Baghai, Coley, & White, 1999)

Keeping all three horizons visible prevents urgent H1 goals from crowding out H3 exploration.

TIP Print the roadmap and pin it beside the performance dashboard. Tag every new KPI or experiment to the horizon it supports.

8.4.2 Embed the brand in company culture

Plans collapse if daily behaviors contradict the promise. Effective brand managers use three habits to turn brand positioning into practice:

1. **Hire for fit:** Include one "living the brand" question in every interview.

2. **Share micro-stories:** Open meetings with a 60-second customer anecdote that demonstrates the promise in action.

3. **Use a brand litmus:** Before approving any project, ask, "Does this strengthen or dilute the brand?"

These rituals make your brand a filter for decisions.

8.4.3 Fund an innovation pipeline

Innovation keeps the brand fresh across horizons, but it needs protected funding. Aaker (1996) recommends allocating 5–10% of brand revenue for H2 projects (adjacent growth) and 1–2% for H3 "moon-shots." Maintain a small portfolio of ideas at different risk levels so one winner can underwrite many small bets.

Example: LEGO's Venture Studio green-lights about 50 ideas each year. Fewer than 5% of those ideas reach shelves, yet those launches now contribute hundreds of millions in annual sales (Christensen, 2022).

8.4.4 Anticipate and mitigate five common brand risks

Decades of brand equity can vanish overnight. Most crises fall into five categories (Table 8.9). Brand managers should build a one-page playbook for each.

Table 8.9   **Five common brand risks**

Risk category	What can go wrong	Early-warning signal	Core mitigation
Product quality/ recall	Faulty batch, safety issue	Spike in returns or support tickets	Batch tracking, rapid recall script
Reputation & social backlash	Offensive ad, influencer scandal	Sudden sentiment drop	Pre-approved apology templates, rollback switch for creative
Supply-chain disruption	Raw-material shortage, weather event	Rising lead times	Dual suppliers, social posts communicating delays.

Risk category	What can go wrong	Early-warning signal	Core mitigation
Regulatory change	New labeling or privacy law	Trade-association alerts	Compliance task force, legal brief library
Leadership misconduct	Ethics breach, lawsuit	Media enquiry	Crisis communications team, interim spokesperson plan

POINT TO REMEMBER
Drafting playbooks when times are calm lets brand teams execute, not improvise when pressure hits.

8.4.5 Run a continuous review cycle

Long-term strategy is not "set-and-forget." Once a year, brand managers should think of the three Rs: Retire, Raise, Refresh.

1. **Retire:** KPIs that no longer signal success.
2. **Raise:** targets that have become too easy.
3. **Refresh:** creative assets so the brand stays culturally current while core symbols remain intact.

This annual audit closes the loop between everyday agility (Section 8.3.4) and multi-year direction.

Throughout the journey from Chapter 1's foundations to Chapter 8's dashboards, you have learned that brand management is a combination of craft and cadence. Craft in shaping identity and promise, cadence in measuring, learning, and adapting. Your next step is to put the frameworks into practice, turning every small decision into proof that your brand deserves a lasting place in people's lives.

Chapter Summary

- Brand health rests on three linked rings: awareness, loyalty, and equity. Weakness in one drags down the next.

- Awareness: Track unaided/ aided recall, SOV, SOS, reach, and impressions to confirm if buyers notice you.

- Loyalty: Watch repeat-purchase rate, CLV, NPS, and advocacy to see if customers return, spend, and promote.

- Equity: Use perception surveys, price-premium gaps, brand valuations, and sentiment to measure name value.

- A quality-vs-price map shows if product or message gains translate into justified premiums.

- Five data feeds—CRM, brand-tracker surveys, digital analytics, social listening, and sales/POS—flow into one dashboard.

- Run the Level–Trend–Relationship (LTR) check to spot which dials need action.

- Fix issues fast with five-step micro-experiments: spot drift, hypothesize, tweak one lever, test, keep, or rollback.

- Scan the external environment with PESTEL, competitive layers, and culture trends to catch shifts early.

- Innovate only around proven customer needs—product, message, or experience—to stay relevant.

- Reserve repositioning or full rebranding for big market shocks; rely on small, agile tweaks the rest of the time.

- Keep a sense–decide–act–learn loop running so the brand adapts weekly, not yearly.

- Plan across three horizons (today, next-wave, moon-shot) so future bets survive day-to-day pressures.

- Make the brand real inside the firm through hiring, stories, and a quick "brand litmus" on every decision.

- Allocate 5-10% of revenue for near-adjacent innovation and 1-2% for long-shot ideas.

- Prepare playbooks for five common crises: product faults, social backlash, supply shocks, regulation, and leadership missteps.

- Close the loop yearly: Retire stale KPIs, raise easy targets, refresh creativity, and keep the brand ready for the next cycle.

Quiz

1. **Which awareness metric tests whether consumers name a brand first without any prompt?**

   a. Aided recall
   b. Unaided recall
   c. Reach
   d. Share of Voice

2. **"Share of Search" indicates _____.**

   a. Media spending power
   b. Intent-driven interest in a brand
   c. Social-media engagement
   d. In-store shelf presence

3. **Net Promoter Score (NPS) is calculated as:**

   a. % Detractors – % Promoters
   b. Average rating ÷ total responses
   c. % Promoters – % Detractors
   d. Repeat purchases ÷ total customers

4. **If a customer spends $40 per order, buys three times a year, and stays four years, their CLV equals:**

   a. $120
   b. $160
   c. $360
   d. $480

5. An advocacy rate of 25% means that:
   a. One in four brand conversations is an unpaid recommendation.
   b. 25% of customers have churned.
   c. Paid ads drove 25% of impressions.
   d. Reach rose by a quarter this month.

6. A brand with a high price premium but very low emotional-equity scores is likely _____.
   a. Poised for margin expansion
   b. Living on borrowed time
   c. Over-invested in awareness
   d. Under-priced versus rivals

7. On a perceived-quality-versus-price map, brands in the upper-right quadrant typically have:
   a. Weak equity
   b. Balanced inventory
   c. Strong equity
   d. No pricing power

8. In the Level-Trend-Relationship (LTR) scan, a change that persists for three straight periods should prompt managers to:
   a. Ignore it.
   b. Note it only.
   c. Investigate lightly.
   d. Prepare an action plan.

9. A micro-experiment loop is designed to:
   a. Revamp an entire brand in one step.
   b. Test one lever for 2–4 weeks and measure one outcome.
   c. Replace long-term strategy sessions.
   d. Guarantee a 10% sales lift.

10. The first step of the five-step micro-experiment loop is to:
    a. Choose a lever.
    b. Lock in results.
    c. Identify the drift.
    d. Form a hypothesis.

Answers

1 – b	2 – b	3 – c	4 – d	5 – a
6 – b	7 – c	8 – d	9 – b	10 – c

Case Study 1: Segment Focus for the Trail Lite Launch

The following case study will give you a chance to apply the customer-segmentation ideas introduced in the "Knowing Your Customer" section of Chapter 2 and to test whether a proposed target market is strong enough to carry a new product line.

Overview

NatureBoots has built a small but loyal audience for its flagship, full-grain leather hiking boot. Founder Isla Tavares now wants to release Trail Lite, a lighter model aimed at day-hikers. Limited capital restricts the launch to one primary segment, and choosing the wrong audience could tie up inventory for months.

NatureBoots

The company sells mostly through its own website, with a handful of specialty shops carrying inventory on consignment. Revenue last year was just over CAD $4 million, generated by a mix of urban millennials who like the brand's eco-friendly leather and seasoned outdoor enthusiasts who appreciate the lifetime-repair promise. Marketing spend is lean and highly digital, relying on targeted social ads and a network of regional hiking clubs.

Proposed Segments

Pre-launch research points to three possible clusters. First are social-media "influencers," young hikers who buy attractive gear that photographs well. They spend less per order and return boots more often, but they generate buzz. Second are "enthusiasts" in their forties who log serious kilometres on multi-day treks and have the highest average order value. Third are "safety-focused day hikers," mid-career adults who hike less challenging trails yet prioritise traction after several high-profile accident stories. Early surveys show all three groups are interested in a lighter boot, but Isla can fund marketing to only one of them for the first twelve months.

Launch Constraints

Factory capacity caps the first production run at twelve thousand pairs. Trail Lite must hit a sell-through rate of seventy per cent in the first two quarters to fund a second production order and keep cash flow healthy.

Case Assignment

1. Using the four-dimensions of segmentation from Table 2.1, evaluate whether the three clusters are truly distinct and reachable.
2. Select the single segment you would target first and explain your reasoning in one concise paragraph.
3. Write a three-sentence value proposition for Trail Lite that speaks directly to the chosen segment.
4. Choose one primary marketing channel for launch and one metric you would track in the first ninety days to confirm product–market fit.

5. Describe one contingency plan if sales lag in the first quarter, and explain how you would decide whether to activate it.

Case Study 2: BrewUp Coffee - Converting Viral Attention into Sales

The following case study will let you practise the performance-measurement tools from the "Managing Brand Performance" section of Chapter 8 by diagnosing why a spike in awareness has not translated into revenue.

Overview

BrewUp Coffee Roasters runs thirty-eight cafés across Ontario and operates a growing e-commerce subscription business. Six weeks ago, a short TikTok clip of its new gravity-fed cold-brew dispenser went viral, attracting nearly two million views. Website traffic more than doubled, and unaided awareness in regional tracking rose from roughly one-third to almost one-half of coffee drinkers.

BrewUp Coffee

Before the viral moment, the company's online store converted about three-and-a-half percent of visitors, with an average order value of thirty-four dollars. Subscriptions, which represent BrewUp's highest-margin product, accounted for one sale in five. The marketing team expected the surge in traffic to lift both conversion and subscription numbers, yet neither moved as forecast.

Post-Viral Challenge

Despite record site visits, the checkout-completion rate slipped below three per cent, and average order value fell by seven dollars. Subscription sign-ups barely budged. CMO Devon Yi believes a friction point exists between curiosity and purchase, but hard evidence is needed before the team rewrites the funnel or reallocates budget.

Current Metrics

Internal dashboards show higher bounce rates on mobile, a longer time-to-checkout on desktop, and an uptick in abandoned carts that include single bags of limited-edition beans promoted in the viral clip. Customer-service emails suggest some shoppers were surprised by shipping costs that appear only at the final step.

Case Assignment

1. Apply the Level–Trend–Relationship questions from Chapter 8 to identify which metric drift poses the greatest threat to long-term brand equity, and explain why.

2. Formulate a clear hypothesis for the low checkout-completion rate; state your reasoning in two or three sentences.

3. Design a simple micro-experiment to test your hypothesis. Specify the single variable you would change, the test duration, the success metric, and the rule for rolling the change out or rolling it back.

4. Suppose the experiment lifts checkout completion by one percentage point but reduces

average order value by two dollars. Using the Awareness → Loyalty → Equity sequence, argue for or against full implementation of the change.

5. Outline a monthly cadence for repeating micro-experiments so BrewUp builds a steady "sense–decide–act–learn" rhythm without overloading staff.

References

1. Aaker, D. A. (2014). *Aaker on branding: 20 principles that drive success*. Morgan James.

2. Aaker, D. A. (1991). *Managing brand equity: Capitalizing on the value of a brand name*. Free Press.

3. Aaker, J. L. (1997). Dimensions of brand personality. *Journal of Marketing Research, 34*(3), 347–356.

4. Bargh, J. A., & Chartrand, T. L. (2000). The unbearable automaticity of being. *American Psychologist, 54*(7), 462–479.

5. Beverland, M. B. (2009). *Building brand authenticity: 7 habits of iconic brands*. Palgrave Macmillan.

6. Binet, L. & Les, P. (IPA, 2020). "Share of Search: A Leading Indicator of Share of Market."

7. Chauhan, R. (2025, February 28). 15+ Social Proof Examples To Help Reduce Bounce Rate of Website. TaggBox. https://taggbox.com/blog/social-proof-examples/

8. Christensen, C. M. (2016). *Competing Against Luck: The Story of Innovation and Customer Choice*. Harper Business.

9. Cialdini, R. B. (2007). *Influence: The psychology of persuasion* (Rev. ed.). Harper Business.

10. De Luce, I. (2019, August 21). What Coca-Cola ads look like around the world. Business Insider. https://www.businessinsider.com/what-coca-cola-ads-look-like-around-the-world-2019-8Duhigg, C. (2012). *The power of habit: Why we do what we do in life and business*. Random House.

11. Farris, P. W., Bendle, N. T., Pfeifer, P. E., & Reibstein, D. J. (2010). *Marketing Metrics: The Definitive Guide to Measuring Marketing Performance* (2nd ed.). Upper Saddle River, NJ: Pearson Education/FT Press.

12. Festinger, L. (1957). *A theory of cognitive dissonance*. Stanford University Press.

13. Fripp, G. (2023, May 16). *Five ways to reposition a brand -*. Perceptual Maps. https://www.perceptualmaps.com/five-ways-to-reposition-a-brand/

14. Fournier, S. (1998). Consumers and their brands: Developing relationship theory in consumer research. *Journal of Consumer Research, 24*(4), 343–373.

15. Goodwin, K. (2009). *Designing for the digital age: How to create human-centered products and services*. Wiley.

16. Holbrook, M. B., & Schindler, R. M. (2003). Nostalgic bonding: Exploring the role of nostalgia in brand relationships. *Journal of Consumer Behavior, 3*(2), 107–127.

17. Johnson, G., Scholes, K., & Whittington, R. (2005). *Exploring Corporate Strategy* (7th ed.). FT/Prentice Hall.

18. Kahneman, D. (1973). *Attention and effort.* Prentice-Hall.

19. Kapferer, J. N. (1992). Strategic brand management: New approaches to creating and evaluating brand equity. Kogan Page.

20. Keller, K. L. (2013). *Strategic brand management* (4th ed.). Pearson.

21. Kotler, P., & Keller, K. L. (2016). *Marketing Management* (15th ed.). Pearson

22. Lafley, A. G., Martin, R. L., Rivkin, J. W., & Siggelkow, N. (2015). "Bringing Science to the Art of Strategy." *Harvard Business Review*, 93(9), 56–66.

23. Lemon, K. N., & Verhoef, P. C. (2016). Understanding customer experience throughout the customer journey. *Journal of Marketing*, 80(6), 69–96.

24. Lindstrom, M. (2010). *Brand sense: How to build powerful brands through touch, taste, smell, sight & sound.* Free Press.

25. Lindstrom, M. (2010). *Buyology: Truth and lies about why we buy.* Crown Business.

26. Lovelock, C. H., & Wright, L. (2002). *Principles of Service Marketing and Management* (2nd ed.). Upper Saddle River, NJ: Prentice Hall.

27. McDonald's Corporation. (2003–2008). Annual Reports. McDonald's Corporation. https://corporate.mcdonalds.com/corpmcd/investors/annual-reports.html

28. McKinsey & Company. (2019). *The Agile Marketing Organization.*

29. Morgan, R. M., & Hunt, S. D. (1994). The commitment-trust theory of relationship marketing. *Journal of Marketing*, 58(3), 20–38.

30. Murphy, E., Illes, J., & Reiner, P. B. (2008). Neuroethics of neuromarketing. *Journal of Consumer Behavior*, 7(4–5), 328–336.

31. Nielsen (2009). "Budgeting for the Upturn: Share of Voice vs. Share of Market."

32. Nielsen. (2021). Global Trust in Advertising Survey. Nielsen. https://www.nielsen.com/insights/2021/global-trust-in-advertising

33. Ogilvy, D. (1983). Ogilvy on advertising. Crown.

34. Osterwalder, A., Pigneur, Y., Bernarda, G., & Smith, A. (2014). *Value proposition design: How to create products and services customers want.* Wiley.

35. Pine, B. J., & Gilmore, J. H. (1999). *The experience economy: Work is theatre & every business a stage.* Harvard Business School Press.

36. Plassmann, H., O'Doherty, J., & Rangel, A. (2010). Appetitive and aversive goal values are encoded in the medial orbitofrontal cortex at the time of decision making. *Journal of Neuroscience*, 30(32), 10799–10808.

37. Plassmann, H., Ramsøy, T. Z., & Milosavljevic, M. (2012). Branding the brain: A critical review and outlook. *Journal of Consumer Psychology*, 22(1), 18–36.

38. Porter, M. E. (1980). *Competitive strategy: Techniques for analyzing industries and competitors.* The Free Press.

39. Porter, M. E. (1996). *What is strategy?* Harvard Business Review, 74(6), 61–78.

40. Reichheld, Frederick F. "The One Number You Need to Grow." *Harvard Business Review,* 81 (12), 2003, pp. 46–54.

41. Schmitt, B. (1999). Experiential marketing: A new framework for design and communications. *Design Management Journal, 10*(2), 10–16.

42. Thaler, R. H., & Sunstein, C. R. (2008). *Nudge: Improving decisions about health, wealth, and happiness.* Yale University Press.Thomke, S. (2020, March 1). *Building a culture of experimentation.* Harvard Business Review. https://hbr.org/2020/03/building-a-culture-of-experimentation

43. Tikkanen, A. (n.d.). *David Ogilvy.* In Encyclopaedia Britannica. Retrieved November 21, 2024, from https://www.britannica.com/biography/David-Ogilvy

44. Veblen, T. (1899). *The theory of the leisure class: An economic study of institutions.* Macmillan.

45. Vigneron, F., & Johnson, L. W. (1999). A review and a conceptual framework of prestige-seeking consumer behavior. *Academy of Marketing Science Review,* 1999(1), 1–15.

46. *Welcome to Dunkin': Dunkin' donuts reveals new brand identity.* Dunkin'. (2025, April 2). https://news.dunkindonuts.com/news/releases-20180925

47. YouGov. "Indonesia: Ramadan Advertising Awareness in 2022." YouGov RealTime Omnibus, 30 Mar 2022.

48. Zanni, GA. (2024, December 27). Cartier's Outdoor Advertising Campaign: A Shining Example of Luxury Marketing. https://ca.bmoutdoor.com/info/Cartier-Luxury-Outdoor-Advertising-Campaign-Toronto

Reference Books

Brand Management Essentials takes readers through every stage of building a brand. The titles below supplement this journey via research, frameworks, and practical examples that reinforce the book's lessons.

Blindsight: Matt Johnson & Prince Ghuman

Want to know why certain cues stick in our heads? Johnson and Ghuman walk through the brain science behind attention and memory. This is invaluable when you're shaping stories that need to hit home.

How Brands Grow: Byron Sharp

Sharp backs every claim with data, challenging common marketing myths. His findings on reach and mental availability line up neatly with the measurement and growth sections in the final chapters.

The Mom Test: Rob Fitzpatrick

Teaches readers how to remove bias from customer interviews and test ideas with real evidence.

Start with Why: Simon Sinek

Sinek argues that people back brands with a clear reason for being. His focus on purpose supports the textbook's opening chapter, where a strong "why" sets the tone for everything that follows.

Buyer Personas: Adele Revella

Revella breaks down how to interview real customers, spot patterns, and turn raw insight into usable personas. It's a natural next step after the segmentation work in Chapter 2.

Positioning: The Battle for Your Mind - Al Ries & Jack Trout

Complimenting the positioning tools outlined in Chapters 3 and 4, this is a classic that teaches how to carve out mental space in a crowded market.

Designing Brand Identity: Alina Wheeler

Wheeler turns strategy into color palettes, tone of voice, and touchpoints customers recognize instantly. Use it alongside Chapter 5 when you're translating theory into concrete experience.

Glossary

A/B split: The process of testing with two different approaches to understand which performs better.

Aided recall: Remembering a brand only after seeing a cue such as a logo, slogan, or product category.

Advocacy: Voluntary promotion of a brand by satisfied customers through word-of-mouth or social media.

Audience segmentation: Dividing a target audience into smaller groups that share common traits such as age, values, or buying habits.

Brand audit: A systematic review of all brand touchpoints to judge consistency, perception, and competitive standing.

Brand equity: The extra value a familiar brand name adds to a product beyond its functional features.

Brand identity: The visible and verbal elements (logo, colors, voice, personality) that signal what a brand is and stands for.

Brand journey: The path customers follow from first awareness of a brand to repeat purchase and advocacy.

Brand loyalty: A customer's ongoing preference and repeat purchase of a brand over competitors.

Brand positioning: The specific place a brand occupies in a consumer's mind relative to rivals based on key benefits or attributes.

Brand purpose: A brand's deeper reason for existing beyond profit, often tied to social or environmental impact.

Brand reputation: The overall public judgment of a brand's quality, reliability, and ethics.

Brand strategy: A long-range plan that aligns brand goals, target segments, and messaging to business objectives.

Case study: A real-world example used to demonstrate how a brand solved a problem or delivered value.

Customer lifetime value (CLV): The total revenue a company expects to earn from a single customer over the entire relationship.

Customer persona: A semi-fictional profile that captures a segment's demographics, motivations, pain points, and goals.

Customer Relationship Management (CRM): Software that stores and analyses customer interactions, sales, and support history.

Differentiation: How a brand sets itself apart from competitors through unique benefits, features, or emotional appeal.

Emotional equity: The extra value created when customers feel a strong personal connection with a brand.

Engagement rate: The share of an audience that interacts with brand content through likes, comments, shares, or clicks.

Gap analysis: Comparing what customers expect with what a brand currently delivers to locate performance shortfalls.

Geographic segmentation: Grouping customers by physical location, climate, or urban–rural setting.

Key Performance Indicator (KPI): A metric chosen to track progress toward a strategic brand or business goal.

Loyalty program: A structured incentive system that rewards repeat purchases or brand engagement.

Market expansion: Growing a brand by entering new regions, categories, or customer segments.

Net Promoter Score (NPS): A 0-10 survey rating that gauges how likely customers are to recommend a brand; used as a loyalty indicator.

Pain point: A specific problem or frustration that a customer wants solved.

PESTEL analysis: Scanning Political, Economic, Social, Technological, Environmental, and Legal factors for external threats or opportunities.

Perceptual map: A perceptual map is a visual positioning tool that shows how customers view your brand compared to competitors based on key attributes.

Perception survey: Research that measures how consumers view a brand's quality, relevance, or personality.

Persona overlap: When two customer personas share similar traits, risking confused messaging.

Price premium: The extra amount customers are willing to pay for a branded product over a generic alternative.

Psychographic segmentation: Grouping customers by values, attitudes, interests, or lifestyles.

Purpose-driven branding: Building brand identity and actions around a socially meaningful mission.

Reach: The number of unique individuals who see a piece of brand content.

Repeat-purchase rate: The percentage of customers who buy again within a set period.

Repositioning: Adjusting a brand's promised benefit or target segment to stay relevant in a changing market.

Retargeting: Serving ads to people who have already visited or engaged with a brand's website or content.

Sales (POS) data: Point-of-sale information showing what, where, and when customers buy.

Share of search: The proportion of online searches in a category that mention a specific brand.

Share of voice: A brand's percentage of total industry advertising or media mentions.

SMART goal: A goal that is Specific, Measurable, Achievable, Relevant, and Time-bound.

Target audience: The primary group of consumers a brand seeks to reach and serve.

Touchpoint: Any moment a customer interacts with a brand, from ads to packaging to support calls.

Unaided recall: Remembering a brand name without any prompts or visual cues.

Unique Value Proposition (UVP): A concise statement of the distinct benefit a brand delivers better than any rival.

Value Proposition Canvas: A framework that matches customer jobs, pains, and gains with a brand's solutions and benefits.

NOTES

www.ingramcontent.com/pod-product-compliance
Lightning Source LLC
Chambersburg PA
CBHW050343270326
41926CB00016B/3592